Resolving Conflict

Communicators. The most important management skill is communication. The authors of this series are all specialists in the art.

Blank Page To First Draft In 15 Minutes
The most effective shortcut to preparing a speech or presentation
Phillip Khan-Panni

2-4-6-8 How Do You Communicate?
How to make your point in just a minute
Phillip Khan-Panni

"Phillip Khan-Panni 'knows what he knows', expresses it clearly, cleverly and concisely. A must read.
JIM RHODE, CSP, PRESIDENT NATIONAL SPEAKERS ASSOCIATION, USA

Communicate with Emotional Intelligence
Use personal competencies and key relationship skills to influence others and get results
John Eaton & Roy Johnson

Say it with Pictures
Apply graphical communication to transform your personal effectiveness
Dr Harry Alder

Communicators is an imprint of How To Books.
For further details please send for a free copy of the latest catalogue
3 Newtec Place, Magdalen Road, Oxford OX4 1RE United Kingdom

Resolving Conflict

Establish trusting and productive relationships
in the workplace

Shay & Margaret McConnon

communicators

Published by How To Books Ltd,
3 Newtec Place, Magdalen Road,
Oxford OX4 1RE. United Kingdom.
Tel: (01865) 793806. Fax: (01865) 248780
email: info@howtobooks.co.uk
http://www.howtobooks.co.uk

First edition 2002

British Library Cataloguing in Publication Data.
A catalogue record for this book is available from the British Library.

Cover design by Baseline Arts Ltd, Oxford

Produced for How To Books by Deer Park Productions
Typeset and design by Baseline Arts Ltd, Oxford
Printed and bound in Great Britain by Bell & Bain Ltd., Glasgow

NOTE: The material contained in this book is set out in good faith for general
guidance and no liability can be accepted for loss or expense incurred as a result
of relying in particular circumstances on statements made in this book. Laws
and regulations are complex and liable to change, and readers should check the
current position with the relevant authorities before making personal
arrangements.

*We have attempted to acknowledge all known sources. We apologise for any that
have been missed. Please contact us so that we can include an acknowledgement in
the next edition.*

Communicators is an imprint of How To Books.

Contents

Appendices 119

The appendices include a questionnaire to help you discover your preferred conflict management style and a collection of other tools to enable you to turn difficult situations around. There is also a case study showing symptoms of organizational conflict – low morale and a high turnover of staff. The study demonstrates how using the processes and language of the 'steps' enables staff and management to listen, understand and work towards a mutual solution.

Bibliography 139

Futher Reading from How To Books 141

"This book offers many tried and tested approaches to ensure that conflicts are managed so that they are positive and creative rather than a process of discrimination."
SIR JOHN HARVEY-JONES

"Your Conflict Resolution Workshops have given staff a greater understanding of themselves. Consequently we now have much improved relationships within the company and with our customers."
SIEMANS

"Conflict resolution is a big part of my work. The techniques and skills in this book have helped me and my team, freeing up precious time for us to be more productive."
RICHARD SHEARD, CHIEF EXECUTIVE, SALISBURY DISTRICT COUNCIL

About the Authors

 **Shay and Margaret McConnon** spent 15 years in Special education teaching young people who had emotional and behavioural difficulties. They developed programmes to enhance the self-worth of these students and improve their social skills.

These programmes were written up and are now a series of twelve titles ranging form *Conflict Resolution* to *Self Esteem.* They continue to form the basis for many Personal and Social Education Programmes across the English-speaking world.

In 1988 they established *People First* management training and consultancy group that specialises in creating winning relationships in the workplace.

People First is best known for its highly acclaimed *Winning Relationships in the Workplace*™ programme. This uses the latest in organizational psychology and leadership theory to create openness, trust and collaboration in working relationships.

The programme is being used by leading companies in Europe and the USA. The workshops are fully supported by a range of products, including workbooks, profiles, posters, memory cards and games.

Shay is a founder member of the Professional Speakers Association and he speaks regularly at conferences on people issues. His keynotes are content-rich, providing delegates with practical techniques for creating winning relationships in the workplace. He uses magic to illustrate these in a fun and memorable way.

Margaret specializes in one to one work and couple counselling. She is co-author of a range of workshop materials and trains on people issues within education and the service sectors.

Preface

Our differences define our uniqueness – nationality, culture, gender, beliefs, values and our behaviours. From a very early age, we are aware of those differences, with siblings and peer groups. We may have different abilities, talents, and levels of attractiveness or interest. Those differences define mankind, allow progress and contribute to the dynamics of the world.

We are also aware that those differences contribute to conflict in our world. Each of us is likely to experience some degree of conflict, be it personal, professional, national or international.

Why is it that the very essence of being human contributes directly to the varying degrees of unhappiness, distress and destruction?

Each of us has our own unique window on our world, fashioned by our socialization and our place in history. We have our own needs, defined by our values and beliefs. When needs are not met, or are denied to us, we are in conflict.

This book offers an understanding of the nature of conflict and structures, which enable the reader to negotiate a solution.

It aims to remove the mind-reading syndrome, which often accompanies conflict, and to replace it with open communication, trust and respect and a simple structure, which allows all parties to reach the magic of win–win.

Shay & Margaret McConnon

Acknowledgements

Many influences have contributed to the writing of this book. Thanks to our friends and colleagues who have encouraged and supported us in developing the ideas and approaches.

In particular we would like to thank Andy Colehan and John Jerwood for their time, professionalism, friendship and most of all their willingness to challenge.

We are particularly grateful to all the people who have attended our workshops. The shared experiences have contributed greatly to the approaches contained in this book.

We wish to acknowledge all these influences and trust that what is offered in these pages reflects the ideals we share.

Language for Conflict or Co-operation ?

◆ Have you ever slammed a door in rage?
◆ Are you inclined to avoid the issue?
◆ Do you say 'you should' or 'you never'?
◆ Do you get the boxing gloves out every time a row beckons?
◆ Do you sometimes make accusing statements like 'you started it' or 'it's your fault'?
◆ Do you often cover up your real feelings by saying 'it doesn't matter' when it does, or 'I'm fine' when you are not?
◆ Ever been so hurt, angry and resentful that you don't care about the other person, you just want revenge?
◆ Have you ever wished you could handle those difficult people better?

If so, then this book is for you. It will give you some tried and proven ways to prevent and manage conflict in your life. It is written for parents, managers, teachers, students, anyone who wishes to manage differences in open and honest ways without argument or conflict.

Me and my big mouth!

No matter who you are, or where you live, if you are in contact with other people you are likely to face some form of conflict, be it a minor irritation or an earth-shattering row.

The answer to resolving these conflicts is right under your nose, in the words you use. Words enable you to build bridges or create barriers. Words have the power to

◆ heal or wound
◆ unite or divide
◆ create conflict or harmony.

The cost of conflict

Of course we are all different from each other. We have different needs, tastes, opinions, beliefs, preferences and values. The question is, how do we cope with the differences? Are they allowed to get in the way and be the source of conflict, or can we celebrate the differences and view them creatively? Let's look at a few problem scenarios.

Relationship cost

Conflict wastes time and money

Kate finds Pete increasingly distant and hostile at times. She would like to come home from work and chat about her day and hear all about his day, but he comes home wanting to be left alone to unwind. Kate feels excluded, and Pete seems to be spending more and more time in front of his computer.

What needs to happen? Would a good row clear the air? Should they pretend there isn't a problem? What choices do they have? What are the words they need to use to resolve this difference?

Mike wants up-to-date information for the monthly sales meeting. Lisa seldom meets the deadline, complaining that she never has time to collect the data and write a comprehensive report.

Mike is getting increasingly frustrated and angry with Lisa. She feels that Mike is unreasonable and insensitive to her situation. The increasing tension and anger shows in the raised voices whenever this matter is discussed.

They are getting locked into a 'you against me' scenario. What choices do Mike and Lisa have for moving this situation forward?

Cost to the individual

While conflict can be constructive, most conflict is destructive, with time, emotional and health costs. Kate and Pete, Lisa and Mike might argue, retaliate, blame and engage in a war of words. Such power struggles can result in stress, loss of confidence, unhappiness, hostility, withdrawal and even illness.

Cost to the organization

Conflict not only has a high personal cost but it is expensive for your organization. Research indicates that a typical manager loses 25% of the day responding to unhelpful conflict. This is time lost to creative, productive work.

Take a medium sized organization with one hundred managers. Let's assume the average annual salary per manager is £40,000. With managers losing 25% of their time on conflict, the cost will be £1,000,000.

This only accounts for management time. The true cost will include wasted employee time, higher staff turnover, missed opportunities, absenteeism, inefficiency, low morale and poor teamwork.

Conversely of course, people who are skilled at managing conflict are more likely to be perceived as leaders, are more influential, gain respect and co-operation and increase the worth of an organization.

Unmanaged conflict is the largest reducible cost for many organisations and it is usually the least recognized.

Breaking the stalemate

In conflict, there is the danger that people get locked into their own positions, digging their heels in and insisting they get their own way. If this happens, it is stalemate with both sets of needs unmet. It is a *you against me* scenario.

This book is about how to make the transformation from *you against me* to *us against the problem.* It is about giving the reader more behavioural choices in managing differences. It will leave you better equipped to deal with the difficult people in your life. It will show you how to:

- ◆ prevent blow-ups
- ◆ defuse anger
- ◆ build bridges
- ◆ keep your cool
- ◆ resolve conflict for good
- ◆ build better relationships
- ◆ avoid the pitfalls.

Chapter 1

How the View Explains our Differences

In this chapter:

◆ **understand your unique window on the world**
◆ **your view is subjective, partial and likely to be distorted**
◆ **hero or villain – who's viewpoint?**
◆ **opinions are not right or wrong they are points of view**
◆ **seek to understand rather than to change others**
◆ **beware of making assumptions about people's intentions**
◆ **explore different perspectives for richer solutions.**

Without realising it, we can become stuck in how we view things. The first way we look at something is not always the only or the 'best' way. The more ways we can view a situation, the more possibilities we will discover and the more creative we can be.

Where do you see this circle:
◆ at the lower right hand corner of the rear panel?
◆ at the centre of the front panel?

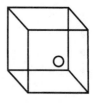

- at the lower right corner of the front panel?
- at the centre of the back panel?

Different views

An old story tells how five blind men once went to find out what an elephant was like. They found one and felt it all over. One found its waving trunk. 'It's like a snake,' he said.

Another found its tail. 'More like a rope,' was his opinion.

A third touched one of the elephant's big ears. 'It's like a fan,' he said.

'No, like a pillar,' said the fourth, feeling its great leg.

The last man leaned against the elephant's massive side. 'It's like a wall,' he declared.

Each of them experienced the elephant from his own point of view, and each came to a different conclusion. That is the trouble with points of view. If you want a true view of anything, you must look at it from every angle. Otherwise, if you stick to your own point of view, as someone has said, you will sit on the point and lose the view.

Beware of expecting others to see what you see We all have slightly different views on the world. Our window on the world is filtered by our early experiences, beliefs and memories. These filters allow us to deal with the two million bits of information that we are exposed to at any one moment. It is impossible to process all this data. So we delete, distort and generalise the incoming information.

However, many of us believe that the way we experience the world is the way it is. It is your unique view … it is the truth for you. Others will have a different view. Their truth, while being different from yours, is right for them.

Your reality is not totality

Of course we don't have totality. What we experience is subjective, partial and likely to be distorted. People believed the world was flat until fifteenth-century explorers discovered that we can go to the East by sailing west. When Albert Einstein was ten years old, his teacher told him that he would not amount to much. Mr Gottlieb Daimler, the founder of Daimler Motor Company, said that the car would never catch on because there would never be enough chauffeurs. The president of Decca Records, rejecting the Beatles, said, 'We don't like their sound and guitar music is on the way out anyway.'

Our views are always restricted to the window we have on our world and its filters. Without realising it, we are discounting something from what is out there.

Which person is the tallest?

'I didn't notice what she was wearing.'
'I didn't realise you felt like that
   about me.'
'I didn't hear him say that.'

How much can you trust your experiences?

Is the world flat? Well it certainly looks it. Is it stationary? It has that appearance. However, the astronomer will tell us we are rotating at thousands of miles an hour. Is the chair you are sitting on solid? If I strike my hand against it, it certainly feels solid. However, the physicist will tell us it is a moving bundle of energy.

Difficult people

Mike is quick to act. Sarah finds him abrasive and Fiona sees him as rash. Who is this person? Is he quick to act, rash or abrasive? He is all three, it depends on the window and the view. They are opinions, each one created from a partial view with information discounted. Who is right? Everyone and no one.

A bucket of water can be a home to a fish, a cool drink to an elephant and a lake to an ant. What you experience reflects who you are. If someone is difficult for you, how much does that reflect you? There will be other people who won't find that behaviour difficult ... they have a different window on it. Maybe people are difficult because of who you are!

Who is right?

Fox-hunting is a sport to some people and slaughter to another. Everyone thinks he is right, and each opinion will be right for that individual. There is always more than what any of us are noticing at any given moment. Expand your view to grow in wisdom.

Can you see the hero?

Because you don't see something, it doesn't mean it is not there. Even though you can't see the stars when the sun comes up, they are still there. You might see this person as abrasive. Behind abrasiveness is quickness to act; this is a strength, even though you might not see it as such. Every villain is likely to be a hero in his own story.

Recognize the positive intention

Conflict often comes from goodwill, people thinking they are doing right but in fact getting it wrong. Having been round the block three times looking for a street, you suggest to your partner that he stops and asks someone … and the advice is rejected. Although you were only trying to help, your partner heard an attack on his competence.

I care – you feel smothered
I am assertive – you see me as aggressive
I am principled – you experience me as stubborn
I am ambitious – you see me as ruthless

Intent and impact

We are inclined to draw conclusions about people's intentions from how their behaviour impacts on us. I feel hurt, therefore you intended to hurt me. I feel put down, so your intention was to humiliate me.

This is not always the case. When someone says *'But I was only trying to help you'* they are really saying they have a positive intention, even though your experience of it was negative.

Beware of making assumptions about people's intentions. You may wish to assume the best about the person, not the worst. In his view he is a hero. Acknowledge this, *'I appreciate you want to help, however, I feel smothered and in future I would like to …'* Now there is the possibility that real understanding and collaboration will ensue.

State your positive intention
Ask yourself what is your real purpose in what you are about to say or do. *'I don't want to waste your time and I'd like to clear up some misunderstandings …'* To enhance co-operation, tell your truth in a way that the other recognizes your positive intention.

Watch your language
While I experience you as abrasive, to say *'You are abrasive'* is unhelpful and likely to lead to argument, as it is not how you see yourself. The view through your window is *'I am quick to act.'*

'You' language is likely to be confrontational. Talk about what you experience about the other person through your window … and don't expect them to have the same view as you!

Do say
'My view is …'
'My perception is …'
'What I experience is …'
'What I need is …'
'My concerns are …'

Beware
'You never ...'
'You are ...'
'You should ...'

Opinions or facts?
In the film *Annie Hall*, Alvie Singer complains
'We never have sex'.
'We're constantly having sex', says his girlfriend.
'How often do you have sex?', asks the therapist.
'Three times a week', they reply in unison.

In conflict we are inclined to treat opinions as if they are facts. Opinions are not right or wrong, they are points of view. They are what you are noticing through that window of yours, which of course, is different to what others are noticing through their windows. Having sex three times a week is a fact. Whether that is too much or too little, is an opinion.

Don't argue with perception	**Truth or importance?** *You drive too fast.* *I deserve a pay rise.*

These opinions are not about what is true but what is important to you. If different things are important to you, these opinions of mine will seem a nonsense and we will just argue. When arguing, I am convinced that I am right and this only distracts me from exploring your world. It is not whether one view is right and another wrong, it is that both views matter. One view is seldom enough.

People who run with the mind set 'I am right' will be inclined to see others as the problem and that they should change ... they are the ones who are being unreasonable, closed and stubborn. In reality, it is the arrogance of the 'I am right' attitude that is likely to perpetuate the problem.

Changing someone

Trying to change someone rarely results in change. Change is more likely to come from understanding. Wanting to change someone implies there is something wrong with that person and of course this only leads to defensiveness and argument. Seeking to understand, suggests the other person is OK in her view of the world. This is the mind set that creates collaboration and mutual problem-solving.

Blame

Blame looks to the past and who was right or wrong. You may wish to keep the focus on the future and how the situation can be solved. When your dog goes missing, where is the energy better spent ... looking for the dog or arguing over who left the gate open? When we feel accused, we can spend the time in futile arguing rather than productive problem-solving. Avoid making the other person wrong.

Sense and nonsense

When we argue, we tend to offer our opinions, use 'shoulds' and give advice.

'You should be more considerate.'
'Slow down.'
'If only you wouldn't be so selfish.'

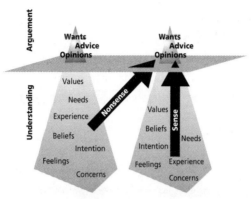

These opinions and advice are like the tip of the iceberg of your thinking. Underneath, and unseen, will be your experiences, beliefs and concerns, from which you form these opinions and advice. They make total sense to you.

However, to someone with a different set of experiences, beliefs and values they become nonsense. Of course, this person will offer different opinions and advice in line with their values, beliefs and experiences.

When we argue, we are likely to be at the tip of the iceberg, trading in the surface thinking of opinions and 'shoulds'.

Understanding is about exploring the unseen bits of other people's icebergs, their thoughts, feelings and intentions. It's about exploring information on themselves that they have access to but that you don't yet see. Arguing drives people apart, understanding draws people together. Rather than contradict a view, you might wish to add to it.

***Explore different perspectives
for richer solutions.***

Chapter 2

Differences in Personality Types

In this chapter:

- ◆ **the four basic personality types**
- ◆ **typical sources of tension across these styles**
- ◆ **strengths can be experienced as weaknesses**
- ◆ **the type that will find your behaviour difficult**
- ◆ **dovetailing the differences.**

Sarah and Mike are driving up the motorway to attend a business meeting. Sarah turns to Mike and asks "Would you like to stop for a coffee?". "No thanks", he answers truthfully. So they didn't.

An atmosphere develops between them, which eventually Mike notices. "Anything the matter?" he asks. "Yes, I would have liked a coffee" and he replies, "Well why didn't you say so".

Communication Styles

Sarah did say so, but in her indirect way. However, Mike has a more direct style and he heard a question of him not a request from her. Mike doesn't understand Sarah. Sarah doesn't understand Mike. It feels as if they don't even speak the same language ... they certainly have different communication styles.

While we may have the same mother tongue, English, somehow we speak different languages. French, English and Italian use the same alphabet but are different languages. Conflict often happens because we are not aware we have different styles of communication, in effect that we speak different languages.

The four Personality Types
Dr Carl Jung in the 1920s studied personality types and described four basic styles. This provides a simple model to understand why people are experienced as different from and difficult for each other. Variations of his model have been validated with hundreds of thousands of people across many cultures, East and West.

Each of the four types has a different way of viewing the world and of communicating with other people. They each have a language

> Difficult people are usually inflexible people

preference. Research shows that people who are fluent across the four languages have most rapport and least conflict. People who are inflexible and locked in their own style are experienced as difficult and the source of conflict.

Go-Getter – Mike
Mike is driven by the need to achieve, to get things done quickly and efficiently. He hates it when his time is wasted or when people take a long time to get to the point. He would not want to be seen as

gullible or indecisive. His communication style is functional and direct. His energy is high and somewhat 'in your face'.

Mike gets straight to the point. He doesn't hold back. If something is a non-runner he says so without any attempt to spare people's feelings. A flaw is a flaw...a spade is a spade. Why waste time on it? So he doesn't. If his colleagues continue to discuss it, he switches off.

Mike is someone who is driven by results. This is how he feels good about himself. He is the 'get it done', 'no problem' type of person. He is a doer rather than a talker or thinker. He is decisive, and even though not all his decisions are the best ones you are likely to hear him say, "you win some you lose some". He believes that indecision is also a decision, and a bad one!

He works to deadlines and likes getting a lot done in a short time. He has little time for small talk and when he rings he likes to get straight down to business. He has little tolerance of people who make excuses or give long-winded explanations and he expects people to keep their personal problems at home. He finds it difficult to listen to peoples' problems.

He would like others to be direct, decisive, to get straight to the point and to be results focused. He respects people who act quickly, take risks and are high achievers. He values success, power and speed.

While Mike sees himself as enterprising, persuasive, decisive and a bit of an entrepreneur, others on his team have a different perspective on him. Sarah finds him arrogant, abrasive, insensitive and conceited. Fiona on the other hand sees him as unprincipled, rash and a risk taker, whereas Darren experiences him as egotistical, inflexible, obstinate and rude.

Carer – Sarah

Sarah is a polite, warm friendly person. She is sensitive, modest and unassuming. She is inclined to take other people's problems to heart and likes to help. Relationships are important to Sarah. She is generous with her time and is a good listener. She feels a certain obligation to volunteer for the jobs that no one else wants to do. She dislikes conflict of any kind and works hard at keeping harmony in the team.

She has a gentle, low-key approach to others and likes to accommodate. She is seldom critical of others and she is usually generous with her praise.

She doesn't want to appear demanding, insensitive or selfish. She is reluctant to be too direct for fear of upsetting others. Rather than express disagreement in meetings, she usually says nothing. This she knows can be interpreted as approval.

She feels Mike takes advantage of her good nature and willingness to please. He delegates the unimportant jobs to her and she feels resentful for being dumped on.

She has been in the same company for 15 years and is known by most of the staff. The main reason, of course, is that she takes the time to listen and enquire about the people and their families and shows sincere concern for them.

She is good at creating a two-way communication flow with the staff and getting people to work together in co-operative, harmonious ways. People feel valued by her and know she is genuinely interested in them and their issues.

Many people appreciate her thoughtfulness, loyalty, cooperative spirit and her sensitive, generous nature. However, Mike sees her as gullible and submissive, Fiona finds her smothering and illogical and Darren experiences her as hypersensitive and subservient.

Mike blames her for spending too much time with people and for being too soft with them. "Time is money and you are wasting it". He feels she should be more business than people focused. He gets angry when she accepts the blame when things are not right.

Sarah finds Mike arrogant, even hostile and doesn't feel his insensitive approach gets the best from people. He is dismissive of her efforts in bringing people together to feel part of a team. She would not want to socialise with Mike outside of work and recognises that she has to work hard to tolerate him as a work colleague.

Analytical – Fiona

Fiona is a perfectionist, and for her getting things right is more important than caring or being successful. She is thorough in her work, paying attention to detail. She is fair, principled and does not like taking risks.

She is adept at building highly effective processes that produce consistent results. This sees her accused of excessive regulation and a 'do it by the book' mentality. She keeps a tight rein on things. She is reluctant to delegate or give control to others, as they may not have her high standards.

Although not regarded as a people person, Fiona does not like to see people treated unfairly. She tends to be prudent and would prefer not to make a decision than make a wrong decision. She has charts posted that show process flow details, check lists and data inventories.

Mike gets frustrated by her 'rather be safe than sorry' attitude. He finds her nit picking, slow and pedantic. He complains about her negativity, always noticing the problems and what can go wrong.

He says it is as if every morning someone programmes her for the working day ... she never deviates from the routine. You could set your watch by her movements. "If she spent as much time doing as she does making lists she wouldn't need a list."

Fiona would like Mike to put things in writing and give her time to think. He expects her to give an answer straight away. She gets frustrated when he gives her work at the last moment and still expects it to be done on time. She sees Mike as rash, compromising on standards and a bit of a gambler.

Fiona doesn't need praise and can feel patronised easily. Sarah is reluctant to work for her as she is big on criticism and small on compliments. Fiona is a solitary person who likes her own company. She is often criticised by Sarah for not being a team player and for her aloofness from people's problems. Sarah finds her difficult to relate to, reserved, cold and unfriendly. Sarah regularly invites her to staff social gatherings and if she doesn't refuse, she will be the first to leave. It's as if she does not need people.

Fiona is suspicious of Sarah's decisions, which are based on intuition and feelings rather than logic and evidence. She is critical that Sarah creates dependency by being too willing to help others. She reasons that this only prevents people learning from their mistakes.

Fiona does not tolerate sloppiness of any nature. She will even make a fuss about a comma missing in a report. People complain that she always seems to find something wrong with everything, that for her, things are always black or white, right or wrong.

Darren at times finds her unimaginative, inflexible, humourless and tunnel-visioned. He wishes she would be more open minded and more open to change.

Socializer – Darren

Darren is a relaxed, easy-going sort of person who can be accepting of delays, changes to schedule and open to new ways of doing things. He is a positive, enthusiastic person who likes a bit of excitement. He is a bit of a free spirit who often ignores protocol.

He likes to be consulted by others in the team and would not want to be seen as rigid, inflexible or narrow-minded. He likes variety and wants things to be different. He becomes bored easily.

Darren is often in the limelight. He doesn't like being confined to routines and get restless in long meetings. He tends to be a dreamer and looks beyond the mundane and the practical. He is inclined to focus on broad generalisations rather than on hard facts. He is open-minded and often changes his mind when new ideas are presented.

The first thing Darren did when he joined the company was to request flexitime and take control over his day. He did not want to be trapped in a routine of having every day the same, and being obliged to do what someone else expected of him instead of stepping to the beat of his own drum.

Darren has creative flair and vision. He can function in chaos and confusion and is innovative in problem solving. People admire his ability to coordinate several projects at once.

Darren is playful and fun-loving. He loves the company's social gatherings where he mixes well and is often the life and soul of the party.

People appreciate his energy especially when work is tough. Somehow he sees the positive in even the darkest situation. He has a knack of generating enthusiasm in people and making crisis moments fun – "What good is worrying, just enjoy it".

Fiona does not always appreciate his humorous slant on life nor does she share his "work should be fun" ethos. Darren thinks aloud, putting his ideas on the table. This annoys Fiona as she likes ideas thought through and justified.

She is upset at his disorganisation and the way he can jump from one topic to another. She wishes he would use less superlatives and was not so unconventional. To her he is frivolous and superficial. She is critical of his meetings, which usually start late and are casual and unstructured.

Darren wishes she would lighten up and be more tolerant of others and their mistakes. He feels restricted by her conservatism and he finds her narrow-minded. She just does not bring out the best in him.

Mike finds Darren's need to consult everyone, time consuming. He gets frustrated because Darren starts several projects at once and then leaves them unfinished to begin even more. Mike needs Darren to be more focused, more decisive, to make up his mind and then stick to it.

While Sarah is fond of Darren and enjoys his company she can find him irresponsible, changeable and she can't always rely on him.

Accommodating to the Style

So here we have four people who are very different from and difficult for each other. It is almost as if they are from different planets. Why? Because they have different drivers, different values, different styles. Mike feels good when he can

Problem solve rather than argue.

achieve, Sarah needs to care, Fiona is driven to get things right and Darren seeks variety. Each has strengths and these strengths can be experienced as weaknesses by other styles.

One or a combination of these basic styles drives us all. We can use all of them at different times but feel most comfortable and good when using our own style.

It is not that one way is right and the others wrong. It is that all styles matter and need to be accommodated. Know your drivers and you will know who will be difficult for you and why others will find your behaviour difficult.

The values need not be in conflict, they can dovetail and blend to create something powerful and effective. Mike's drive combined with Sarah's sensitivity, Fiona's methodology and Darren's creativity will be a powerful force in any organization.

This happens when people recognize the validity of each other's style. In the naive state we argue and conflict. We are convinced that we are right and the other wrong. Alternatively we can problem solve and use the steps from chapter 7 to create win-win, dovetail strengths and be special.

It is as if we are from different planets!

Chapter 3

Fight the Difference or Celebrate it?

In this chapter:

◆ **conflict is more to do with style than substance**
◆ **whether conflict really is constructive**
◆ **how rows can spiral out of control**
◆ **the three basic choices in managing differences**
◆ **stages leading to relationship breakdown**
◆ **how 'shoulds' can be a cancer to relationships**
◆ **win-win is about meeting both sets of needs.**

Every day in the media we hear or read about war, violence, divorce and social unrest. Talk to your friends and they will tell you about their rows, arguments and difficult people. Your children will argue over the TV and you may even have experienced road rage.

Some people see conflict as a game, a combat sport and they look for sparring partners. Others can be devastated by the merest tiff.

Is conflict inevitable? Is a relationship without conflict healthy? Is harmony even desirable? Is conflict always bad and to be avoided?

Is conflict inevitable?

Conflict is not inevitable simply because we are different. We can disagree and not be in conflict. Conflict is more to do with style than substance. It happens because of what we do and say about the differences, rather than arising from the differences themselves.

> The differences don't have to get in the way

Conflict starters

The escalation or diffusion of conflict is to do with style, the words and the emotional energy used. There are a number of ways that conflict can esculate.

'Typical of you.'
'No wonder you didn't get that promotion.'
'You should take more pride in your work.'
'Why can't you be more like your sister?'

Blame
Accuse
Interrupt
Patronise
Contradict
Exaggerate
Personal insults
Hostile language
Bring up the past
Make assumptions
Use labels or put-downs
Don't accept what the other person says
Use 'you never…' 'you always…' 'you should…'

Circumstances can escalate the conflict

Issues that are resolved in minutes on that sunny beach in the middle of that relaxed holiday, can turn out very differently if you both have had a hard day, it is late in the evening and the children won't settle!

Things that can turn a trivial issue into a major disagreement include:

◆ tiredness
◆ stress
◆ insecurity
◆ illness
◆ mood
◆ alcohol

Conflict is complex

We might be arguing about money but the real issue may be about control. That sloppy report which is handed in late might be to do with a lack of recognition and a feeling of being taken for granted.

When a minor incident erupts into a major row, there is likely to be a deeper, more complex issue at stake. The screwdriver left in the wrong place, the toothpaste squeezed in the middle, the car parked at an angle ... suddenly you feel you have walked on a landmine – you probably have! The row is not about the screwdriver or the car but a deeper unfulfilled need ... perhaps to be valued, to be involved, to be accepted.

As the issue is hidden, we may not be conscious of what it is that is upsetting us until we talk about it. Until people talk about and discover the underlying need, they will be dealing with the symptoms, patching things up, becoming more frustrated and growing apart.

Little hurts

Have you ever noticed how a small graze or cut finger can really hurt when you brush against someone? Without the sore, it would have gone unnoticed. When life is going well, we also have a buffer, which protects us in the small 'brushes' with life. If the little conflicts of life hurt deeply, it may be useful to notice any other sore or deeper issue. Deal with causes not symptoms.

Is conflict constructive?

Many people suggest that conflict is healthy and constructive. While conflict can provide broader perspectives and deeper understanding, for most people conflict is destructive.

A conflict is constructive only if as a result:
◆ the relationship is stronger
◆ you understand each other more
◆ there is greater willingness to meet each other's needs
◆ there is greater trust
◆ you have resolved the source of future conflicts
◆ there are richer perspectives.

If the conflict results in deeper frustration, negative feelings and a growing hostility, it is destructive to the relationship. You have created a remedial situation from which you have to recover.

How rows can spiral out of control

We don't always see a row brewing. It can catch us unawares. Before you know it, a spark becomes a flame, then a fire, and you don't seem to be able to control it any more.

A slight difference over weekend plans can lead to personal insults, widen to include an attack on in-laws, and suddenly the couple are ready to break up.

It is OK to be different, it is not OK to dysfunction.

(Pete arrives home late from work and tired after a long day).

Kate: Where have you been? You didn't say you'd be late.

Pete: I don't have to account for every minute of my time.

Kate: This is typical, you never consider anyone else.

Pete: You are getting more and more like your mother, nag nag nag ... I wonder why I come home at all.

Kate: So do I ... you just sit in front of the computer expecting to be waited on hand and foot.

Pete: You haven't got a clue.

Kate: You know what your problem is ...

(Pete storms out, slamming the door and shouting).

Road to breakdown

Here are some stages that relationships go through on the way to breakdown.

1 Discussion
This is when both people are interested in the other's view of the world and are prepared to share ideas, opinions and feelings. This stage is simply the meeting of minds with no intention to get the other person to think or feel anything different.

Characteristics include:
◆ respect for each other's viewpoint
◆ acceptance of the other's values
◆ broadening of perspectives

2 Debate
This is when there are different viewpoints and I would like you to see things my way, but only if it is right for you.

Characteristics include:
◆ openness to your ideas
◆ respect for your viewpoint

3 Argument
I want you to 'buy' my ideas, regardless of what you may be thinking. I am 'right' and you are 'wrong'. You should be doing it my way.

Characteristics include:
- ◆ disregard for other's viewpoint
- ◆ arguing from own perspective only
- ◆ polarization
- ◆ lots of 'yes buts ...'

4 Conflict

Not only do I believe I am 'right' and you are 'wrong' but I insist you do it my way that you act according to my values and beliefs.

Characteristics include:
- ◆ demands that you behave, as I want
- ◆ highly personalized arguments
- ◆ lots of 'shoulds'
- ◆ blame, accusation, put-downs

5 Breakdown

The relationship is now so painful that I need to protect myself or recover from the pain. I act as if you don't exist.

Characteristics include:
- ◆ silence
- ◆ 'cold war'
- ◆ separate lives

How far through these stages do you need to go to manage differences in open and honest ways? You may find that argument and beyond are signposts to broken rapport and a deteriorating relationship.

What are the choices?

Each of us is different and special. We have our unique beliefs, values and needs. Different perspectives, viewpoints, goals and approaches are the natural consequence of these differences. The greater the differences, the more difficult it can become to maintain harmony in the relationship.

We have three broad choices when it comes to managing differences.

1 We can choose to discuss and debate our differences, respecting each other's opinion.
2 We can argue about these differences, i.e. we are convinced we are right and the other should have our perspective.
3 We can move into conflict about these differences by imposing our way of doing things.

What drives the conflict?

David delegates to Michael in a detailed, precise way, insisting he follow the procedures that he has decided are right. Michael feels restricted and performs best when he can be creative. He likes to be given a task and the freedom on how to complete it.

Argument

They argue. David argues that getting the job done right means that procedures are agreed and followed. Michael argues that procedures can restrict creativity and demotivate him. In essence David wants something that Michael doesn't value and vice versa.

Conflict

Arguing is 'intellectual'. Conflict is behavioural. Conflict happens when David insists his procedures are followed, preventing Michael from operating in a way that is

> Why do you insist on me seeing what you see, when I don't?

important to him. This is a violation of Michael's needs. The consequence is that Michael will begin to feel *worth less*, be unhappy and less motivated.

Arrogance

While difference lies at the source of this conflict – David needs procedures and Michael needs to be creative – it is arrogance that drives the conflict. Each is convinced he is 'right', *his* way is best and the other 'should' be like him. If the other person was like you, had your beliefs, values and way of doing things you wouldn't be in conflict. The sub text around conflict is: *'I want you like me … you should be like me.' 'I want you to change to me, my ways, my standards.'*

> You are creating the conflict in your life if you are imposing your values on others, denying them, their needs.

> Others are creating the conflict in your life if they are imposing their values on you, denying you, your needs.

We may not recognize that we are denying other people their needs. We are likely to have a positive intention and are doing what we consider 'right' and best.

Rules, expectations and 'shoulds'

If I make value judgements – 'you should' 'you ought' 'you must', I am implying that my way is best for you, that my values are more important than yours. This is both arrogant and disrespectful … it is not accepting that the other person can legitimately value other things.

'I expect you to notice my feelings.'
'I expect you to consult me.'
'I expect you to listen to me.'

We are inclined to expect others to value what we value. Procedures are important to David and he expects Michael to value these too. Our expectations follow on our values and become our 'rules' for life.
When my expectations are not met, when my rules are broken, we are in conflict.

Beware of the 'should'

If I believe my boss should support me in front of others, I will be in conflict with him if he criticizes me in front of my work colleagues. The conflict is happening because of a mismatch between his behaviour and what I expect it should be. Someone who expects the boss to be straightforward in public, if necessary, has different expectations and will not be in conflict because of that behaviour.

Reduce conflict by recognising the positive intention.

Whose rules are right?

Your rules are right … they are right for you, they show the way to meeting your needs and getting what is important to you. But what is important to you won't be for others, their rules are right for them. What will be 'wrong' is to impose your rules on other people and expect them to live by your rules.

Win-lose is when both people are trying to have their needs met at the expense of the other person's. *Win-win* is when both people problem-solve so all needs are met.

Who knows best?
While each of us is 'right' in expecting and needing different things, it is sometimes necessary for an experienced person (boss, parent, or teacher) to determine what is in the other's best interests. This is best when discussion of needs has taken place and an understanding shown for each other's positions.

When Barry was fifteen years old, he wanted to leave school and work as a car mechanic. His father had a different view, he wanted him to go to university. It took some time for Barry to see a different perspective but now he is glad that his father persisted. Today he is the vice-president of a multi-national corporation.

Resolving conflict

As conflict is caused by a denial of people's needs, the successful resolution must involve the satisfaction of those needs, otherwise the conflict could simmer and re-ignite. If you want a lasting win, look for the win for the other.

If Michael just ignored David's need for procedures and does the work his way, his needs are met and David's are not ... it is *win-lose*, 10 for Michael and 0 for David. If David pulls rank and insists that Michael follow his procedures regardless of his need to be creative, this is *lose-win*, 0 for Michael and 10 for David.

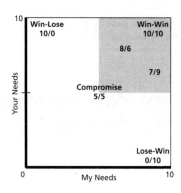

In both these scenarios the conflict remains unresolved and will continue, albeit under the surface, until there is some element of *win-win*.

Conflict resolved in the unshaded area is likely to keep re-emerging as needs are largely still unmet. Try to get a compromise with 5/5 and above. While it may not be possible to get 100% satisfaction, aim for at least 50% + satisfaction for both parties.

Celebrate the difference
The view through your window is different, not better, not right, just different. The difference need not be the battleground, it can be the source for broader perspectives. There is nothing wrong with you and there is nothing wrong with me, but there may be something wrong between us. Celebrate rather than fight the difference.

While differences explain conflict, it is arrogance that drives it.

Chapter 4

Are You Building a Bridge or a Barrier?

In this chapter:

◆ **the resolution mindset**

◆ **the language that fuels conflict**

◆ **bridging enables 'you' and 'I' to become 'we'**

◆ **sharing power does not mean giving up power**

◆ **conditions that lead to win-win**

◆ **the power of co-operation.**

Conflict will escalate or defuse because of your conflict management style. People react to what you say and do. Whether you defend, attack, retreat, appease, you affect how the other will respond. It is a dynamic moment and you control the direction and the final outcome by the processes you use … by how you use your words and energy.

Does this happen?
'I think the best way would be to...'
'Yes but...'
'Yes, but I still think...'
'What you don't seem to realize is...'
'Whatever you say, I think the best approach would be to...'
'Why don't you listen to sense?'

'You're the one being difficult.'
'No I'm not. You're the one with the problem.'

You and me becoming we

To the extent that you are able to translate *me* and *you* into *we*, you will develop affinity, rapport and get co-operation. If you don't, there is the real likelihood of division, frustration and the escalation of conflict.

In conflict, people usually feel under threat of losing something which is important to them. It is this perceived threat that puts them on the defensive and there is little chance of getting collaboration while it remains. A joint solution is more likely to be achieved if the threat, real or imaginary, is removed. To achieve this, focus on the other person with the intent to meet their needs. Attending to what you want, regardless of the other, can create this threat.

> There is nothing to be gained from attacking the other person and everything to lose.

The resolution mind set

It doesn't have to be win-lose. If I win £10, you lose £10. If I have three quarters of the cake, you will only have a quarter. If one person gets the promotion, the other loses out. This win-lose mind set forces you into a competitive attitude and language.

This mind set is appropriate in sports but can miss the point where people are concerned. The win-lose tactic assumes there is not enough for everyone to have what he or she needs. Lisa wants to be in at one in the morning and Dad wants her home by eleven. These times exclude each other. As we shall see later in the book, shifting the perspective from wants to needs, can provide a lot more flexibility in terms of win-win.

A reluctant partner

It takes two to be in conflict and it requires the will of two to resolve the conflict. If you find that the other party is not interested in resolving the conflict, but wants to hurt or win at any cost, then a different approach is necessary. You may need to protect yourself from the conflict, to walk away or to seek a third party intervention.

> People often get in their own way.

To get a more co-operative response you may want to look at how you are perceived. Are you seen as a threat? Are people suspicious of your motives? While this may not be how you see yourself, it could be how you are perceived. You might be OK but others may not see you as OK.

Try a positive statement. Mention your intention. Ask what is needed from you. Talk about the advantage for the other person.

'I would like to find a solution that works for both of us.'
'How do you suggest we go about this?'

However, some people will have more to gain by keeping the problem alive than by solving it. Hence they will be reluctant to work with you.

Win-lose

When winning becomes more important than understanding, it's a *you versus me* scenario. Then, instead of listening, people are likely to be preparing a counter-argument or even a counter-attack!

The win-lose mind set leaks out in the language used. It can become a war of words with lots of verbal bullets.

'Any fool knows …'
'Of all the stupid ideas …'
'The trouble with you is …'
'You must be an idiot if you can't see …'

To get more fire-power, we attack the person *'No wonder you have been passed over for promotion four times.'* When we need some heavy weaponry we bring out some old mortar bombs *'… and it was your fault that we lost the PX contract.'* Hostile language eats up large amounts of time without achieving anything.

> If you shoot from the hip, you could end up with a bullet in your foot.

People can get locked into hostile language patterns. It is as if they know no other way of approaching differences. People who use co-operative language are likely to bridge the differences. Hostile language opens the divide and creates division. Keep the language environment clean if you want people to act from their heads rather than their stomachs. It was Benjamin Franklin who said that any fool can criticize, condemn and complain … and most fools do.

Conflict must be fuelled

People may get into hostility loops, feeding more ammunition and pain into the loop from both directions ... both are struggling for power and are locked into the win-lose mind set. The gap widens and each digs himself into a deeper hole.

Hostility loops have to be fed, they are not self-sustaining. It takes two to argue but only one to stop ... without fuel for the loop, the hostility will splutter and the emotional intensity weaken.

Bridging

You can argue till you are 'blue in the face' but you will lose if you make the other person feel outdone. You can outtalk, outsmart, outwit, outreason but still fail, if the other person does not feel good at the end. Only if the other person's needs are heard and met will it be a win. You win when he wins.

The person you are in conflict with is likely to be more interested in what he needs and wants than in what you need or want.

Bridging is about attending to that person, noticing the needs, concerns and feelings, finding common ground, finding places where *you* and *I* can become *we*, where interests, needs and concerns can be seen as mutual. The more communication you invite, the more you are likely to create the win-win environment. This can be done verbally and non-verbally.

> Don't expect others to collaborate if you go on the attack.

Bridge mind set

- You are OK
- Let's work together
- I want us both to win
- I want power with you
- Your needs are important
- Let's problem-solve rather than argue
- We have a mutual problem to be solved

Some bridging words

- Us
- We
- Our
- Can
- Let's talk
- Appreciate
- Alternatives
- What do you need?
- What do you think?
- Help me understand
- What would you say to...?

Non-verbals

- Soft gestures
- Open posture
- Make eye contact
- Voice low and slow
- Look and act approachable
- Sit or stand at angle of approximately 90°
- Use open hand gestures – palms slightly upturned

Barrier mind-set
- I am right
- You should change
- You are the problem
- I want power over you
- I want to lay down the law
- I want to prove you wrong
- I am indifferent to your needs
- You are wrong and you should be different
- My needs are more important than yours

Some barrier words
- Me
- You should
- Waste of time
- Your problem is
- That won't work
- Out of the question
- That's my final word
- This is non-negotiable
- You don't understand
- I've heard all this before
- You wouldn't understand

Non-verbals
- Frowning
- Lip-biting
- Raised voice
- Arms crossed
- Hands on hips
- Sharp gestures
- Hands in pockets

- ◆ Hands over mouth
- ◆ Avoiding eye contact
- ◆ Narrowing of the eyes

Power with, not over

To share power does not mean giving up power. It can be like sharing the light of a candle. When you light another person's candle, your light does not diminish. In fact there is more light for everyone. The enlightened approach to resolving conflict involves respect. Respect is about recognizing others as being different and accepting them with their differences. It happens when I am able to say *You're OK* even though you have a different set of values and principles from me ... if I accept you for who you are rather than who I want you to be ... if I recognize that your needs, although different, are as important as mine.

> Be partners, rather than opponents.

Win-win is more likely when people
- ◆ focus on both sets of needs, concerns and feelings.
- ◆ respect each other's view.
- ◆ see the issue as a mutual problem to be solved.
- ◆ are prepared to listen and compromise.
- ◆ are not interested in winning at any cost.
- ◆ opt for power with rather than power over.

The power of co-operation
People will not co-operate with you, if you seem to be against them. Aim to be open, receptive and willing to collaborate.

Fight the problem, not the person. Create an atmosphere in which everyone feels that something can be gained, i.e. everyone is a winner. Maybe you don't get what you want until others get what they want.

For me to win, you don't have to lose.

Chapter 5

Understand and Manage your Feelings

In this chapter:

♦ **anger is a signal that something is not right for you**
♦ **understand how you 'do' anger**
♦ **learn to control your anger**
♦ **managing anger in others**
♦ **knowing when to take time out**
♦ **listening is the foundation for agreement.**

Have you ever been so hurt, angry and resentful that you don't care about the other person, you don't even want to resolve the conflict, you just want to get revenge and to hurt? Even 'nice' people can become abusive and threatening in conflict.

Unresolved feelings have a habit of leaking into the conversation. Even when you desperately try not to let your emotions show, they can pop like the cork from a champagne bottle, often with messy results. How can you control these feelings and what can you do to prevent the anger?

Recognize the anger

Feelings are indicators of what is going on in your life. Anger is a signal that something is not right for you. It is your body's way of letting you know that something is wrong, that your values have been violated. Feelings are just another part of you, like your arms and legs and like your arms and legs, they can be controlled.

Venting

While you may have a strong urge to shout, scream, kick, hit or run, acting out of the anger is likely to be destructive to a collaborative relationship. Beware of what you say in the heat of anger. The cross words could constitute the best speech you will ever regret!

Playing your personal stereo at high volume will cause hearing loss of the higher frequencies. Yelling and shouting is also likely to result in hearing loss ... the other person may just 'close down'. A soft and gentle tonality is likely to improve hearing. You may wish to try speaking about your anger rather than speaking from your anger. People who throw temper tantrums are usually not taken seriously.

Suppressing

Anger that is not dealt with can turn inwards and leak out in resentment, bitterness, withdrawal and depression. Suppressed negative feelings can damage your health. While it is easy to suggest you describe and express your anger in a positive way to the relevant person, experience may have taught you it is expedient to settle for surface peace as the lesser of two evils.

Unexpressed conflict is still conflict

Releasing

Suppressed anger is stored in the body. If it is not released it can build to the point where you 'explode' or 'dump' on someone. Find a way that is right for you to manage your stress, otherwise it will act as a toxin to your system and can lead to illness and disease. Talking with friends, sports, meditation, relaxation can all be ways of releasing the stress.

Some people need space to think before they are ready to discuss a conflict. Some need to sort it out quickly. Respect each other's needs and agree a time to talk. Allowing issues to accumulate can add fuel to growing anger.

> I was angry with my friend
> I told my wrath, my wrath did end.
> I was angry with my foe
> I told it not, my wrath did grow.
>
> *William Blake*

Manage your anger

Conflict is often high on emotion and low on reasoning. When the anger 'runs' me, essentially I become more stupid, in the sense that my perspective narrows. I become less rational. The primitive part of the brain takes over. I can't think clearly. I am likely to do and say things I will regret later.

When you get angry, adrenaline flows faster, veins are enlarged, your heart beats faster. The body is equipped for a brawl rather than

Anger can severely limit your choices.

for problem-solving. Where do these feelings come from and what can you do about them?

How do you 'do' feelings?

Whatever you feel, you have a strategy for it. Feelings are a consequence of something you do. Your anger will be related to your thinking, your body and your language. Make an intervention in one or all three areas and you will change the feeling.

Feelings are less to do with the 'real' world and more to do with what you tell yourself about the 'real' world. It is all to do with that unique, subjective, partial view you have.

It is the middle of the night and you hear the floorboards creaking … you are convinced a burglar is creeping up the stairs and you feel terrified. Your feelings are unfounded however, as it was only the stair boards contracting after a warm summer's day.

On another occasion, you again hear the stair boards creaking and you tell yourself that it is only the boards contracting … and you feel calm, even though this time there really is a prowler on the stairs!

Watch your thinking

Feelings follow on from your thoughts. Change your thinking if you want to change your feelings. The thinking behind anger is likely to contain a *you should*.

'You should be more considerate.'
'You should have known.'

Take the *'you should'* out of the thinking and how angry can you be?

Being considerate was a choice he had.

Remember, *'you shoulds'* imply that my way is best for you, that my values, beliefs and methodologies are better than yours. By taking the *'you should'* out of your thinking, you can inoculate yourself from anger. Guilt comes from *'I should'*.

'I should have helped more.'

Take the *'I should'* out and how guilty can you feel? And of course, you run the risk of causing resentment when you tell others what *'they should'* do. Simple as it seems, by taking the *'shoulds'* out of your internal and external conversations, you reduce anger, guilt and resentment.

You may wish to replace '*shoulds'* with *'coulds'*. Rather than say *'I should'* try *'I could'*. Instead of saying *'you should'* use *'you could'* or *'I need'*.

Watch your physiology
Your anger will be reflected in your physiology, your gestures and your voice. It is as if your body contains the anger. Try to be angry without clenched teeth, a high-pitched voice or wagging your forefinger, and you could discover that you can't get as angry. Note how your body is when you are angry and reverse this, e.g. if you find yourself pointing with your right forefinger, next time

put your right hand in your pocket and point with your left hand. Reverse the expression and you diminish the feeling.

> Anger is fuelled by your thinking, your body and your language.

Suggestions for next time:
- ◆ Lower the volume of your voice.
- ◆ Slow the rate of speaking.
- ◆ Use circular rather than linear gestures.
- ◆ Breathe from the stomach.
- ◆ Soften the face muscle.
- ◆ Delay before responding.

Watch your language

Your anger is somehow contained not only in your physiology but also in your language. Rearrange the words for a different experience. Instead of saying *'I'm pi**ed off'* try *'I'm annoyed with you'* or *'I'm disappointed.'* It is as if the anger is in the words, and if I choose less expressive language, I will experience less anger.

Coping with anger in others

What do you do when the other person is shouting and screaming at you? While you may need to protect yourself from anger that is directed at you, recognize that some people need to let off steam before they can begin to move forward. Rather than going on instinct by retaliating or retreating, listen and encourage the venting. In this way you are likely to defuse the hostility and get to calmness and rationality.

'Brake time'

If you validate, listen and paraphrase and yet the other person remains accusatory and abusive, you may wish to separate yourself. It takes two to play. If you don't have a partner you don't have a game! Avoid running or storming out of the situation. Excuse yourself: *'I recognize you have strong feelings about this and I think it would be best if we talk about this after we have had a chance to think things through.'*

> If both of you are yelling, no one is in charge.

When an argument is getting out of hand, you may wish to take a break for half an hour or so to 'cool' down.

'I feel this is getting us nowhere … I'm getting too worked up here … would it be a good idea to take a break and meet again at three o' clock?'

It takes two to fight, one to stop. The bottling up of anger and walking out of the room in a 'huffed' silence is not brake time. Nor is avoiding the conflict, brake time. By giving yourselves time, you take the 'heat' out of the situation to confront the issues more rationally. Brake time is about postponing the talking, not avoiding it. Defuse the anger to deal with the problem.

What not to do

Avoid giving advice or telling the other person to do anything. Although well intentioned, words like 'calm down', 'there's no need to be angry', or 'keep your voice down' are likely to cause resentment and anger.

The sub text in these responses is 'you are wrong to be angry'. Such an invalidation will break rapport.

What to do

1 Validate

Acknowledge what the other person is feeling and recognize it as valid for her.

> Validate the feeling to keep rapport.

'I can see you have strong feelings about this.'
'So you feel ... because ...'

2 Ask the magic question 'what ... ?'

By asking the person what they want you are giving them some control and reducing the feeling of helplessness ... you are creating a *power with* scenario and the need for anger is dissipating.

> People who say sorry don't always forgive.

'What do you need from me?'
'What needs to happen ...?'

3 Check for understanding

Paraphrase to ensure you understand what the person has said. It is difficult to continue to be angry when someone is genuinely trying to understand you.

'So what you are saying is ...'
'If I understand you correctly ...'

Listening is key

Listen without interrupting, arguing or disagreeing.
Accept what they say as their reality. It is their
perception, it is valid for them while it may not coincide
with your perception.

Listen to understand even if there is blame, accusation or
demand, even if as you see it, there are distortions and
exaggerations.

Listening leads to understanding, and understanding is
the foundation for agreement. Conflict grows in the
absence of understanding.

 ***Listening is key to making the
transformation from you against me
to us against the problem.***

Chapter 6

Develop Your Skills and Increase Your Choices

In this chapter:

♦ **recognize your patterns – fight, flight or flow**
♦ **listen to understand the other's view**
♦ **talk constructively about your view**
♦ **problem solve for mutual wins**
♦ **non-verbal communication**
♦ **how to disagree, agreeable**
♦ **the pitfalls of blame, accusation and judgment**
♦ **rules for constructive controversy.**

It's a warm summer's afternoon and the fly in your kitchen is getting more agitated as it tries to get outside. You open the window but the fly doesn't recognize the opportunity and remains 'trapped' in the kitchen. Even when you encourage it with the help of a magazine, it ignores your support and goes back to the familiar spot on the pane of glass.

At times, we can be like this fly, unaware of the opportunities we have, ignoring support and wanting to do things the way we always have. Often we continue with the familiar and the comfortable rather than with what works best.

The fly who 'attacks' the window with even more determination, ends up hurt as well as unsuccessful. This is often the case with people who become aggressive and demanding. If we want a different outcome, go for a different approach. Many of us are great at continuing to do what doesn't work, unaware that we have choices. So what are my choices and indeed what are my current behaviour patterns in conflict?

What's my style?

Whether the tension is about budgets, in-laws, children or sex, people are inclined to respond with pretty much the same patterns. This is usually some form of collaboration, giving in or attacking. Your pattern is likely to take you down a familiar path with each conflict, experiencing the same feelings and getting similar results.

While all styles of dealing with conflict are useful, the best approach depends on the situation you are in and what you want to achieve. There are three main patterns of response:

◆ flight
◆ fight
◆ flow

None of these is inherently good or bad, just more or less effective. While flow creates good working relationships and provides a solution to meet everyone's needs, it presupposes the other person wants to collaborate. If not, you may need to protect yourself or use another style to ensure needs are catered for.

Develop flexibility if you want to increase effectiveness

Just as a golfer plays with a variety of clubs, you may 'play' the course of human differences better with a variety of approaches. It can be restricting to stay with that club or style which is familiar and comfortable to use.

Flight

Peace at all costs.

This lose-win style means saying 'yes' to accommodate the other person. It is usually the pattern for people who value the relationship over the goal. Strategically, this may be an appropriate way of responding. For example, you might decide the customer is always right and agree to his request; or you might be with someone who is unreasonable and you decide to accommodate.

However, the lose-win personality (i.e. when it is a consistent pattern rather than a conscious choice), is likely to lead to frustration, anger with self and the danger of being exploited. You can choose flight behaviour without being a flight personality.

Fight

Attack is the best form of defence.

This is the win-lose style. It involves using power, threats, bluffs, intimidation, anything that will help to win the conflict. This pattern is used by people who value goals over relationships.

Again this may be appropriate as a choice in some contexts. When someone vulnerable is being physically or verbally attacked, you may go into fight mode to protect as a first response. This is fight behaviour driven by caring.

When people are not prepared to flow, you may wish to use this approach. For example, you decide to put pressure on an unreliable person to ensure you are no longer inconvenienced by his late reports.

However, the fight personality only values winning, it is 'power over', and has little regard for the person or feelings. This will result in alienation, isolation and resentment. This person becomes 'locked' into win-lose, as opposed to a person who borrows fight behaviour to achieve a particular relationship objective.

Flow

Lets find a way to... This win-win approach focuses on the concerns of everyone and looks together for ways to reach agreement. This is about standing up for yourself without blaming, accusing, demanding or being hostile. This approach recognizes that both sets of needs are important and seeks solutions to satisfy everyone. This leads to win-win, a sense of *power with*, and positive, collaborative relationships.

To flow is non-combative. It is not backing down or burying your head in the sand pretending there isn't an issue. It is going with the energy, the way an Aikido master will flow with the energy of the other rather than fight it. The aim is to divert the attack by disarming the energy. Aikido looks to align and harmonize. In physical practice, it resembles a dance as the attacker's energy is deflected and rendered harmless.

The win-win approach creates partners, not opponents. It means searching for ways to involve and satisfy everyone. The mind set 'let's see how we both can have what is important to us', shows you are not out to fight, it creates that bridge for mutual gain … it is about respect.

While you may need to borrow fight and flight behaviours when the other person is not prepared to flow with you, it is the flow mind set that leads to the sense of collaboration and solutions built from everyone's needs.

Key skills for collaboration

Here are three skills which prevent the escalation of the conflict and allow you to steer the energy along a path that will increase understanding, trust and co-operation.

1 *Listen acceptingly* – find out what others see through their window on the world.
2 *Talk constructively* – share what you see through your window on the world.
3 *Problem-solve* – marry the views for mutual wins.

1. Listen to understand the other person's view on the world

To view the difference only from my view will be restricting … I will have limited information. Listening to the other person will provide another view, wider perspectives and more possibilities.

Understand first, respond second

As children, we have been taught to be quiet rather than to listen. Listening means you are open to the other person's perspectives, needs and concerns. It is not judgemental, you accept what the other says as valid and 'right' for them, even if you disagree. It involves putting aside any preconceived notions you may have about that person.

Listening can be a bit like reading the newspaper. Something catches our eye and we exclude those bits of the paper that are not of interest. We are also inclined to scan and delete as we listen. Quite unconsciously we can listen selectively and filter out information. We don't always hear what is said, and we don't realize this either.

Listening is judgement free.

Checking with the other person that you have heard correctly is a way to build understanding and giving the other person a deeper sense of being heard. Listen to understand and accept, rather than to justify, judge, advise or argue. By listening in this way you are likely to bring out the best in the other person.

'Help me to understand …'
'Tell me about …'
'Let me see if I understand …'
'Have I got that right?'
'Can you give me an example?'
'How important is this to you on a scale of 0-10?'

It is crucial that you listen for what is important to that person. After all, that is why the conflict is happening … because something which is important to that person is being denied. You may just find that it is impossible to continue to be in conflict when someone is trying to understand you and meet your needs.

> 'Yes buts' indicate argument rather than listening.

Listen for feelings
Feelings can wander around the conversation looking for some acknowledgement to hook on, and once hooked, can somehow fly off and disappear in space. Without validation and air space, feelings can get in the way and block the communication flow.

'I'm annoyed that you lied to me.'
'It was only a little white lie.'

This responds to the substance of what is being said, not the feelings. Here is a way to get the feelings into the conversation.

'I'm annoyed that you lied to me.'
'It seems as if you are really upset about this.'

Remember, while you may not agree with the substance of what the other person is saying, you can still acknowledge the importance of feelings. Often, people don't feel listened to until their feelings have been understood.

When Frank says he will spend Sunday afternoon with Susan who feels neglected, he thinks he has not only listened to Susan, but has also dealt with the problem. However, the real issue is her feelings … she needs to have her feelings aired, explored and validated. Only then will she feel that Frank really understands her.

Not everyone is like Susan. For some, the solution will be the answer. Give the Franks of this world a 'fix it' approach and understanding to the Susans. Some people will want a mixture of both. People don't always want to be treated in the way you do.

> Giving the solution is not always the answer

Listen to understand

'I feel neglected'
'There's no reason for you to feel neglected'
'What you should do is…'

Whilst these reactions may be understandable, they don't deal with the real issue or allow the person to feel understood and accepted. With understanding, the problem often 'melts' away. Incredible as it may seem, 70% of people's problems need no other solution than understanding.

Here are some questions which will help understanding.

'What lets you know you are neglected?'
'What do you need from me so you wouldn't feel neglected?'
'Can you help me to understand what it is like to feel neglected.'

> Take turns in having equal 'air time'.

How not to do it

Karen: I have such a headache. *(explains situation)*

Samu: Do you want a paracetamol? *(wants to help)*

Karen: I've already taken two. *(shares her solution)*

Samu: You try to do too much, why don't you lie down. *(advises with positive intention)*

Karen: I don't want to lie down, I've too much to do. *(rejects the advice – gap widening)*

Samu: That's daft. Anything you have to do can wait. *(justifies advice already given – polarisation begins)*

Karen: Will you stop trying to sort me out. I said I don't want to lie down. *(reacts to advice – gap widens further – resentment)*

Samu: Your problem is you are stubborn, just like your mother. *(accusation – hot button fired – issue widening)*

Karen: And you are a typical male. Just leave me alone and stop telling me what to do. *(stereotyping – feels misunderstood – sense of hopelessness)*

Karen does not feel listened to and feels annoyed with Samu for giving her advice. Samu feels that not only has he listened to Karen (how could he give advice unless he first listened?) but he has had her best interests at heart. He is feeling confused and hurt as she has rejected his 'help'.

Samu was listening to Karen but not listening to her in a way that would allow her to feel listened to. It is not enough to listen, people must know you have listened.

◆ Understanding changes the expectations.
◆ Understanding leads to fewer demands.
◆ Understanding is the foundation for agreement.

Mishearing is the norm

We use words to describe ideas, feelings and needs. But the words are not the experiences, no more than the photo is the person it represents or the brochure is the product it describes. Words are the 'wrapping paper' for our experiences. My wrapper might contain chocolate but you might think it wraps toffee. 'I need more appreciation' might be heard as 'you want a pat on the back' but what I really need are bigger challenges.

What you hear may not be what was actually said. Language is an imperfect way of communicating thoughts and feelings.

For accuracy, check what is inside the wrapper and ask for specifics.

It's a pity we speak the same language, because we don't!

'What specifically do you mean?'
'In what way, exactly?'
'Can you give me an example?'

Paraphrasing

Beware of assuming that people hear what you say or that you hear what the other person says. While you hear the words spoken you may not give the meaning to the words that the person intended. George Bernard Shaw said that the problem with communication, is the illusion that it has taken place. Mishearing would appear to be the norm, and then people argue over what was never said. To improve accuracy, let the other person have the floor and every so often sum up in your own words what you have heard. This not only allows you to hear accurately but shows that you are making a serious attempt to understand and get the other's view on the world.

'So what you are saying is …'
'What I am hearing is …'
'Say more about that to help me understand …'
'Is there anything else you want to say?'

People who say they haven't got time to listen are really saying they don't yet value listening enough to give it the time required. They are also implying they have time for the consequences of not listening, which are misunderstanding, argument and conflict.

Listening gets you into the other person's view.

Listening starters

Here are some open questions to get the person talking about the differences. Accompany these with a gentle tone of voice and open body language, so they are heard as invitations to speak.

'What are you angry about?'
'What do you need from me?'
'What are your concerns?'
'What needs to happen so it is right for you?'
'How do you see it?'
'Say more about why this is important to you.'

The voice in your head

Often we can be distracted by what's going on inside … our internal conversation. Sometimes this can be so 'loud' and judgemental it is hard to 'hear' the other person.

'How can he say that?'
'Here we go again!'
'This is all the thanks I get.'

There may be plenty you are thinking and feeling but not saying. Aim for a positive internal dialogue which enables you to focus totally on the other person.

> Listening makes a lot of sense.

Acceptance listening

1 For the moment, put to one side your concerns, feelings and needs.
    ◆ Focus on the other person.
    ◆ Seek his view on the world.

2   Listen for what is important to the other person.
   ◆ Be genuinely interested.
   ◆ Encourage her to talk.
   ◆ Explore her feelings, needs and concerns.

3   Accept what the person says as true for him.
   ◆ Resist argument.
   ◆ Suspend judgement.
   ◆ Recognize his right to say something even if you
   disagree with it.

4   Every few sentences, sum up what you have heard.
   ◆ 'So what you are saying is …'
   ◆ 'What I am hearing is …'
   ◆ 'Anything else you want to add?'

5   You are not listening acceptingly if you
   ◆ justify
   ◆ argue
   ◆ advise
   ◆ judge
   ◆ interrupt

> Rather than create a one way street, drive on a communication highway, where ideas and feelings can pass freely in both directions.

2. Talk constructively to share your view on the world

How do you tell the other person that you feel put upon, misunderstood or that you are hurt and angry? People who are 'honest' in expressing themselves can find it backfires … they end up rowing and further apart. It is not just a question of being honest, you must be honest in skilful ways.

> 'Drawing on my fine command of language, I said nothing.'
> Robert Benchley

To open with *'I am angry with you because ...'*, can be provocative, as the underlying message is 'you are wrong'. Such openings may be how you are viewing the situation but they contain value judgements and imply the other person is at fault.

More openness will be created by acknowledging the differences and seeking to understand the other person's perspective.

'We seem to have different approaches to ...'
'Help me to understand why you want to ...'
'Would it be a good idea to talk about ... ?'

People who talk constructively, express thoughts, feelings and opinions in honest, open and straightforward ways. Remember, you are sharing your view on the world and on this person's behaviour in particular. This is partial, subjective and filtered. It is your opinion and the other person will have a different opinion. You may see the person as a villain. He will see himself as a hero.

When things don't go right, we're often quick to blame. This is especially true if we have been storing up resentment and anger. Blame the other person and they are likely to blame you.

'You only think of yourself.'
'It's all your fault.'

> Avoid character assassination

To avoid making the other person wrong, talk about yourself and how that person's behaviour affects you. Using 'I' language rather than 'You' language can prevent the situation getting personal.

Avoid
'You are...'
'You never ...'
'You should ...'
'You always ...'
'You don't ...'
'You make me feel ...'
'Why can't you ...'

Say
'I feel ...'
'I'd prefer ...'
'I'd like ...'
'I need ...'
'My concern is ...'
'I don't like ...'
'I believe ...'
'As I see it ...'

Talking starters

You risk not being heard if you try getting your message across indirectly, through humour or sarcasm. Beware of expecting others to read your mind ... tell people what is important to you and what you need. Here are some sentence starters to enable you to be not only direct but respectful.

'I am angry that …'
'I want …
'I am sad that …'
'I need …'
'I am sorry that …'
'I wish …'
'I am concerned that …'
'What is important to me is ….'
'As I see it, what this is really about …'

Beware 'Never' and 'Always'

Often we speak in exaggerated terms, especially when
feelings run strong.

'You never come home on time …'
'You always forget to call …'

Does he never come home on time? It might feel he never
comes home on time but it probably is an exaggeration.
You are likely to be taken more seriously if you make
accurate statements or talk feelings: *'It feels as if you never
come home on time' 'It feels as if you always forget to call.'*

Instead of saying, *'You are never at home'*, it will be less
provocative if you say, *'I feel neglected when we are not at
home together.'*

Rather than saying, *'You are always late'* try this: *'When I
am kept waiting, I feel unimportant.'*

Try something like, *'When I sense I am excluded from the
decision-making process'* rather than *'You never involve me*

in decision-making.' 'Always' and 'never' will always (well almost always!) shift the focus away from the real issue. You have created a diversion and probably something else to row about.

Share feelings

Often we confuse being emotional with expressing emotions. You can express emotions well without being emotional and you can be extremely emotional without expressing much of anything.

To say *'I am angry with you because ... '* may provoke a response *'And I am angry with you ...'* with each person getting angrier.

This is happening because people are feeling blamed. It will be more helpful to keep the focus on yourself and what you are feeling. *'I feel angry inside, I'm worried and confused and I need to feel we are at one on this.'*

Talk to the relevant person, not everyone else.

Talk in positive terms

Ever notice how when you go on a diet and you decide not to eat chips and cream cakes ... what do you become obsessed with? Yes, those chips and cream cakes just won't leave your mind.

The mind doesn't seem to be able to handle negatives except as positives e.g. don't think of a pink elephant and what do you get ? How big is your pink elephant! Beware of saying things which are negative – *'I don't want us to fall out over this'* or *'This is going to be difficult.'* You may just end up getting what you don't want! Keep focused on what you both want rather than on what you don't want. Otherwise it will be like the golfer who says to himself as he is about to strike the ball, *'I don't want to hook the ball.'* The chances are, he will hook the ball precisely because of what he is telling himself. Talk about what you want rather than what you don't want.

Past or future?

Talk future not past. It will usually be best to talk about how you want things to be rather than what has led to the present conflict. While accepting that some people need to come to terms with a situation by talking about the past, this can also trigger bad feelings and often leads to arguing, blame and accusation.

Non-verbals

Strange as it may seem, your body is part of the conversation. Research indicates that over 70% of any social interaction is non-verbal. Your body, which is never 'silent', communicates attitudes and feelings. This 'commentary' is likely to be 'louder' than the words.

Here are some guidelines to receptive, open body language:

1 Look at the person.
    ◆ A stare can threaten.
    ◆ Looking down or away can be interpreted as lacking confidence.

2   Speak in a calm, friendly and controlled tone of voice.
  ◆ Breathe deeply.
  ◆ Avoid mumbling.

3   Match the other person's energy and state.
  ◆ This will aid rapport.

4   Beware the following:
  ◆ arms and legs crossed.
  ◆ hands covering mouth.
  ◆ body facing away from the other person.

If you have a win-win mind set and genuinely want to meet the needs of the other, your non-verbals are likely to automatically communicate openness and receptivity.

> Your body is doing a lot of the talking!

Validate

Besides expressing negative feelings, talk about what you appreciate in that person. Recognize the positive intention and what he is trying to achieve. Validate the viewpoint, needs and intention. Say *'I know you are trying to save us money by repairing the washing machine yourself, however I have been without the machine for a week and I need to have clean clothes for the family'* rather than *'This is typical. You can never do anything right. I knew we should have got a service engineer to do the job.'*

Interruptions

When someone interrupts you and won't let you finish, you may wish to use some of the following control techniques.

Closing your eyes, putting your hand up and looking away are some non-verbal ways for getting control. It is best to combine these with expressions like *'Please let me finish'* or *'Hear me out.'*

Really, you want the other person not only to hear but to be open to what you are saying. If you first listen to them in non-judgemental ways, you are more likely to be listened to.

Guidelines
Here are some guidelines to enable you to express your view on the world and keep a collaborative relationship for win-win.

1　Talk solution rather than problem:
   ◆ Speak about how you want things to be rather than dwell on the past, what has happened, who said what etc.

2　Avoid any hint of blame, judgement or criticism:
   ◆ Beware of words like *'You should ...'* *'You never ...'* *'You make me feel ...'*

3　Talk about what you observe and see rather than what you think or believe:
   ◆ Say *'When talking to you and I don't get eye contact I feel you are not interested'* rather than *'You are not interested.'*

4　Feedback on the behaviours, never the person:
   Talk about the behaviour being a problem for you rather than imply the other is a problem person ... after all the behaviour is not a problem for them.

◆ no personal comments
◆ no mind reading
◆ no assumptions

> Solution pointing rather than finger pointing.

5 Use 'I' language:
By talking about your truth rather than implying you have the truth you are less likely to appear hostile or accusatory.
◆ *'The way I see it …'*
◆ *'My perception is …'*

6 Offer your support and collaboration:
◆ Make it obvious that you want to be part of the solution.

7. Use feedback to inform:
◆ Beware of using it to advise, blame or demand.

8. Recognize the positive intention:
◆ Assume the best and give the benefit of the doubt.

3   Problem-solve for mutual wins

Identify needs
If the listening phase does not lead to a resolution, it will be necessary to negotiate and problem-solve. The listening is likely to identify a variety of unmet needs. List these and decide on one to work with, as it is unwise to work with several issues at once.

If people don't take time to explore needs they may deal with wants or symptoms instead of with the root cause.

This is a form of patching things up and leads to continued frustration and the re-emergence of the conflict in the future.

Brainstorm solutions

List several ways to meet both sets of needs on this issue. Aim to get 5 – 10 alternatives. At this stage it is best not to criticize, judge or evaluate the suggestions … so no 'yes, buts'. Encourage wacky or way out ideas, anything to keep the creativity flowing. Evaluation of these ideas will come in the decision-making phase.

Beware of the quick fix.

Decide a way forward

Look for what you have in common. Talk about what you agree about. Create a *yes* rather than a *yes but.* Go through the list and mark anything that both of you are open to. This will narrow the options. Discuss the positives and the negatives of each remaining option. As you talk you are likely to have more choices than was originally thought.

Use currencies in which you both can trade i.e. a win for both of you. You may, in your give-and-take approach, offer things which are easy for both of you to give. Aim for minimal cost and maximum gain. An 'elegant' currency is one which is low cost for one person and is of high value to the other.

Agree a plan of action

It is best if this plan is written down and check whether both people understand and agree to it … who will do what …

Agree before you disagree

how and by when. Being specific can prevent confusion. Set a review date to see how it is working out.

More choices

Beware of the tit-for-tat scenario which only leads to stalemate and lose-lose. If you want people to listen to you, to look for areas of agreement and to meet your needs, first listen to them, look for agreement and seek to meet their needs. While their behaviour is likely to follow yours, there are no guarantees when it comes to people. But generally behaviour breeds behaviour.

How to agree
If you agree with the other person, confirm it by saying what you liked and why you like it, or you may appear patronising.

How to disagree
If you just counter with a different viewpoint without first validating what the other person has said, you may lose rapport and create a *you versus me* situation. Although some people like the directness and don't have an issue with counter-arguing, you are more likely to maintain rapport if you:

◆ validate the idea
◆ express your reservations
◆ seek alternatives and problem-solve

> View objections as unfulfilled needs.

> Jeff: What I like about your idea is that the report will be shorter *(validate)*
>
> What concerns me is that the key sales figures will not be emphasised *(reservations)*
>
> What can we do so the key sales information is there without making the report longer? *(problem-solve)*

Arguing

'Yes buts' often indicate argument mode. Arguing is more likely to polarise than to persuade ... people digging their heels in and defending their own positions. People become locked into their own view and are less open to persuasion. If you 'win' the argument, you are likely to have lost the mind and heart and there is no sense of collaboration or understanding. Arguing is win-lose; problem-solving is win-win.

Arguing is a poor persuasion technique as you will be arguing from your own logic and value system. People move for what is important to them, not what is important to you. Make the links to the other person's values, if you want to influence and persuade.

Respond rather than react

Here are some examples of responding positively to concerns and objections. These open questions allow you to reframe the resistance and keep rapport.

It will never work.	**What do you dislike about it?**
My way is better.	**What makes that seem the best option?**
It's impossible.	**What would it take to make it possible?**
I can't.	**What difference would it make if you could?**
You can't do that.	**What would happen if we did?**
That is not the best way.	**What would be the best way for you?**
It's too expensive.	**Compared to what?**

Rules for constructive controversy

Here are some guidelines for keeping the discussion free of blame, accusation and judgement.

◆ Be critical of ideas but not the person.
◆ Listen to understand, not to win.
◆ Recognize all viewpoints as valid.
◆ Be open to new perspectives.

It may be useful to put yourself into the shoes of an observer, someone with no stake in the issue, someone who understands that both sides have valid concerns and can give an objective perspective on moving forward. As this person, what would you say to each of the individuals? How would you comment on their negotiating styles? What would be your suggestions for moving the situation forward?

Not getting what you want can be a wonderful stroke of luck.

93

Negotiate

1 Listen acceptingly:
   ◆ Show you understand.

2 Look for what you can give to the other person:
   ◆ Meet real needs.
   ◆ Listen to objections and concerns and incorporate these into the agreement.
   ◆ Look for ways to help this person save face.

3 Ask for what you need from the other:
   ◆ Express your concerns and needs.
   ◆ Be prepared to give and take.
   ◆ Look for ways that you can save face.

4 Make it a fair deal:
   ◆ Ensure there is maximum win for both people.
   ◆ Check needs are met.

 The most significant journey of your life may be to meet someone halfway.

Chapter 7

Four Steps to Resolution

In this chapter:

◆ **the importance of understanding and meeting needs**

◆ **attend to the other person first**

◆ **explore the need behind the want**

◆ **invite the other's solution**

◆ **build for maximum win-win**

◆ **fast track to collaboration**

◆ **dealing with power plays**

◆ **the steps guarantee you will manage differences without conflict.**

It was 8.30 in the evening. The lights in the restaurant were dim and music was playing softly in the background. We were browsing through the menu, when we noticed a couple across from us.

They were having coffee after their meal. He had his arms folded tightly, a scowl on his face and staring angrily at the ground. She had her back to him and was blowing cigarette smoke aggressively into the air.

Suddenly, she broke the silence. 'That's always been your problem. You click your fingers and expect people to jump to attention ... even the children don't like you.'

Out of embarrassment, I dug my head deeper into my menu as he retorted, 'You are getting more and more like your mother. I don't know why I ever married you'.

The menu was a blur as out of the corner of my eye, I saw her throw the remains of her coffee over him. He grabbed her tightly by the wrist and through clenched teeth said, 'Don't ever do that again'.

Goodness knows what I ordered that night! He eventually released his grip and they sat back to back, in angry silence. Ten minutes later they left.

Imagine if I was daft enough to follow them and ask: 'How much do you feel understood by your partner 0-10?' The answer is likely to have been '0'. 'How much do you feel your partner is willing to meet your needs 0-10?' The answer is likely top be '0'.

It is impossible to escalate conflict when people are trying to understand each other and meet each other's needs.

The steps

While there is more than just one way to resolve any conflict, there are certain processes that will enable you to manage the differences in open and honest ways without damaging the relationship. Here are four steps, using the skills from the previous chapter, that allow you to make the transformation from *you against me* to *us against the problem.* This model has evolved through work on conflict management in organizations and couple counselling.

Steps one and two show that you are trying to understand the other person.

Steps three and four show that you are willing to meet their needs.

Step one

Attend to the other person

'Your presentation was too detailed and too long.'
'Yes, but the board needs all the data if it is to make an informed decision.'

When we are criticized or given feedback, the majority of us are likely to justify and explain our actions. After all, we are intelligent people, we have thought out the situation and we do things for reasons.

> Beware the 'yes but ...'

> Leroy: You don't listen to me!
> Tanya: But I do.
> Leroy: No you don't, you just keep on working. You don't even look at me.
> Tanya: Yes, but I can listen to you and work at the same time.

While Tanya felt she was listening to Leroy, that was not his experience. Tanya was not listening to him in a way that allowed him to feel listened to.

Justify if you want to start an argument, validate if you want to keep rapport.

Defending yourself only makes things worse. If, as a first step, you ...

◆ justify
◆ retaliate
◆ explain your situation
◆ talk about what you want

... you are likely to widen the gap and create a barrier. Of course your situation is important. Talk about your situation only after you attend to the other person's viewpoint and feelings. In this way you improve understanding and create a sense of collaboration.

What to do
The first step in resolving conflict is to attend to the other person and validate the opinion, feeling or intention. To validate does not mean to agree. It is the acknowledgement that the person's thoughts or feelings are OK ... it is her reality. For example:

'How would you want the presentation to be?'
'What lets you know I don't listen?'

Most of us get locked into our own situation; focus on what we want and need, and are less inclined to consider the other person's needs.

When we have an unmet need, there is pain. The greater the pain, the more we focus on ourselves and our needs. If you lie awake all night with pain from toothache, you know how difficult it is to be altruistic and think of others when you hurt so much. In conflict, there are unmet needs, there is pain ... expect people to focus on themselves. Reverse this if you want to create a collaborative relationship.

Some attending questions

By attending to the other person as a first step, you are likely to minimize resistance, create a feeling of being listened to and begin to build that all important bridge.

'What needs to happen so it is right for you?'
'What do you need from me?'
'What can we do about it?'
'What would you like to see happen?'

The answer to these questions will tell you what the other person wants, i.e. the solution to his unmet need. If you can meet this solution there will be no need to negotiate or go further on these steps.

> *Leroy:* You don't listen to me.
> *Tanya:* What would let you know I listened to you?
> *Leroy:* Look at me instead of continuing to work on your keyboard.

If Tanya can give Leroy her full attention, then there is a solution which is acceptable to both of them. There is no need to go beyond this step.

Step two

Explore the need behind the want

Mike wants to have up-to-date information for the monthly sales meeting. Lisa regularly fails to meet the deadline, complaining that she wants more time to collect data and write a comprehensive report. They both want different things and the wants exclude each other. Neither of the stated solutions work for the other person.

If Lisa and Mike stay at the level of wants, they will argue, counter-argue and get more frustrated with no progress being made. It will be a *you against me* scenario.

The want or position taken is seen as a specific solution to a need or interest. Asking a *why* question will flush out the need that is driving the want.

Lisa needs to do the job perfectly, Mike needs information so next month's sales targets can be agreed. Perfection and deciding sales targets may not exclude each other.

At the level of needs both people can problem-solve, negotiate and make real progress.

> Wants are solutions to needs.
> Wants often exclude each other.
> Wants are driven by needs.
> Needs can be met in ways other than the expressed want.

Questions to reveal the need

By exploring the need behind the want, not only will you keep the focus on the other person, you will intensify the feeling of being listened to and deepen understanding.

'Why is that important to you?'
'Why does that matter?'
'Why do you want that?'

Step three

Invite the other's solution

The danger with giving our own solution is that it is designed from our criteria and view of the world and may not match the needs of others. It can be like giving someone your glasses, which have been prescribed for near-sight to someone who suffers from far-sight.

Be solution focused

Use the *what* question to move from the problem to solution. There is the danger if too much time is spent on the problem, negative feelings will be triggered and a sense of hopelessness created.

Problem-solve on both sets of needs e.g. Mike might ask Lisa, *'What needs to happen so you can maintain your standards and the team agree sales figures?'*

Some problem-solving questions

How would you see us solving that?
What do you suggest?
What would be your solution?

'What can we do so you get … (your need) and I get … (my need)?'

Inviting the other's solution leads to a sense of *power with* and collaboration. Because the person is involved in designing the solution, you are more likely to get commitment to this rather than compliance.

Step four

Build for maximum win-win

In the same way as you wouldn't knock a wall down in your house without checking why it was built, you may not want to knock an idea without first understanding why it was suggested.

The solution offered may not be as bad an idea as first appears. Madame Curie had a 'bad' idea that turned out to be radium. Richard Drew had a 'bad' idea that turned out to be Scotch tape. It will be useful to recognize the validity of what is offered and then express your concerns. By building on what is offered you can reach an acceptable agreement.

Lisa may suggest that Mike delegates some of her work, freeing up time. If this solution does not meet Mike's needs, he may help Lisa to think through the consequences of this suggestions and negotiate further. The conflict is not resolved until there is a win for both people.

'What I like about your suggestion is...'
'My concerns are...'
'What do you suggest we do?'

You against me

Peter: Hello James, what can I do for you?

James: I feel I deserve an increase in my salary to reflect my commitment and the hours I've worked in recent months. *(want)*

Peter: We have had a difficult year, sales are down and targets have not been met. Regrettable as it is, I must say no. *(own situation)*

James: Yes but I need more money ... I can't make ends meet. *(reiteration of position – feels unheard)*

Peter: You don't seem to realize – my hands are tied. *(frustration – feels unheard – gets locked into own position)*

James: And you don't seem to realize what it's like to scratch a living from the pittance this place pays. *(anger – polarisation of positions)*

Peter: You are just being unreasonable now. *(accusation)*

James: And you ... *(slams door)* ... Oh, what's the point? *(gap growing)*

This escalates for the following reasons:
◆ Peter's opening response was to explain his situation rather than attend to James and his needs.
◆ The interaction stays at the level of wants ... needs were not explored (I want more money – more money is not available – how many times do I have to tell you).

◆ It is *you against me.* It is *'I want'* versus *'you can't have.'*

The outcome is that neither feels listened to or understood. They are angry and frustrated and the relationship has deteriorated. The issue will smoulder and is likely to resurface some time in the future. A barrier rather than a bridge has been created.

Us against the problem

Peter:	Hello James, what can I do for you?
James:	I feel I deserve an increase in my salary to reflect my commitment and the hours I've worked in recent months. *(want)*
Peter:	If I were to increase your salary, what would that do for you? *(attend – explore needs)*
James:	I would feel my contribution was recognized and I'd feel more valued. *(feels listened to)*
Peter:	So a salary increase would enable you to feel more appreciated. *(feels understood)*
James:	Yes.
Peter:	We've had a difficult year, sales are down and targets have not been met. *(my situation)* What can we do so you'd feel more appreciated considering we don't have

	the money to support a salary increase. *(validation – invite solution)*
James:	I suppose if I was given more responsibility I'd feel more appreciated but I'd still like my salary to be reviewed at the earliest opportunity. *(solution)*
Peter:	If we agree to talk salary in three months time, would that work for you? *(check for agreement)*
James:	Yes.
Peter:	What sort of responsibility did you have in mind? *(focus on other)*
James:	I'd like to head up the next project. *(want)*
Peter:	You certainly have a lot of relevant experience.
James:	I would need …
Peter:	What do you suggest … ? *(build)*

This works because Peter

- attends to James as a first step.
- flushes out needs.
- invites James to give the solution.
- builds.

> Work on the relationship as well as the problem.

The result of this approach is that James feels listened to and understood, he senses a willingness by management to meet his real needs. He is being taken seriously and his needs are partially met. Although the circumstances are identical in both scenarios – James wants a salary increase and money is not available to support this – a bridge has been built and the relationship strengthened.

You will create conflict if you do not consider the needs of the other person.

Fast track to collaboration

> *Sheila:* Your department never produces its reports on time. *(want)*
>
> *Sean:* It isn't a perfect world. We have problems here I can't always control. *(justification)*
>
> *Sheila:* Yes but what you don't realize is ... *(argument)*
>
> *Sean:* And what you don't seem to understand is ... *(polarisation)*

Of course there are reasons why the reports were not ready. To merely explain why they are not ready is likely to damage the relationship and create *you versus me*. If you wish to create the collaborative *us against the problem*, include some form of validation and problem-solving. The following example demonstrates how using the third step alone can achieve this.

> *Sheila:* Your department never produces its reports on time. *(want)*
>
> *Sean:* I appreciate deadlines are important, *(validation)*
> however it isn't a perfect world. We have problems here I can't always control. *(my situation)*
> What can we do to ensure that the inconvenience to you is kept to a minimum considering the fluidity of my situation? *(problem-solve)*

Old habits

Sometimes you will use these steps while the other person continues in old habits of blame and attack. It can seem as if you are getting nowhere. Even so, it is possible to have a productive discussion:

Naomi: I've been thinking about what happened and I am concerned how it might affect our relationship. I'd like to understand what was going on for you and share my view on things. *(invite)*

Mark: The problem was your attitude, you blindly rush into things. *(attack)*

Naomi: You feel my attitude was unhelpful. *(acknowledge)*
Can you say more about this? *(focus on other)*

Mark: The truth is you shouldn't have said what you did. You make me really angry when you don't think things through. *(accuse and blame)*

Naomi: Sounds like I really got it wrong for you. *(validate)*
What would you have needed from me? *(invite solution)*

Mark: Well, for a start, I'd like you to …

Naomi: Why is this important to you?

STEP 2

Mark: … *(answer)*

Naomi: My situation is … what can we do so you get … and I get ….

STEP 3

As you will probably require the patience of a saint to maintain this process, it may be as well to balance the amount of patience needed against the value of the relationship to you.

Power plays

What can you do with the stubborn person who is dismissive of your needs and is not prepared to compromize? You can be passive, you can fight, or you may wish to confront this person with their behaviour and invite discussion of it.

Here is a way of being assertive while keeping a sense of collaboration. It enables you to begin a conversation without any hint of blame, accusation or demand. It is in three parts:

> Never give up on anybody. Miracles happen every day!

1 *The behaviour* – a non-emotive description of the current behaviour
2 *Your response* – how you feel or think about the behaviour
3 *The preferred behaviour* – what you would need instead

*'When I sense my needs are being dismissed
I feel angry
And I would like us to work in more collaborative ways.'*

If the other person continues to dismiss your needs e.g. 'You are over-reacting', you can loop again on your assertive request.

'I appreciate you feel I am over-reacting
However, I feel dismissed
And I would like us to work in a more collaborative way.'

This three-part formula is a conversation opener. The discussion is only beginning and it is off to a good start. You still need to explore each other's views and problem-solve for mutual wins.

Real life

While it makes sense to follow the steps sequentially, a real life conversation is interactive, with people moving up and down and off the steps. The steps are designed so that whatever step you are on, you have access to all the other steps. A productive conversation may require you to go from step one to step three, back to two and so on. Staying on the steps and climbing back on will always be an option!

Language of the steps

View the language given with each step as a suggestion. It may be useful to develop your own style and words while retaining the process.

> Ending a relationship can be an assertive option.

Let the needs of the other person determine how long you spend on each step. People who come to terms with their problems by talking through their feelings and needing to feel understood, will appreciate delaying on the first two steps. Those who require solutions rather than understanding, will want to move quickly onto the problem-solving stages.

Use the ideas and examples from the previous chapters to help you with this. Paraphrasing can be used with any of the steps to ensure accuracy.

Different styles for different personalities.

Guarantee

The tennis coach does not guarantee you will win your matches after you have had a series of tennis lessons. The coach provides you with more choices and flexibility in your game, increasing the possibility of winning.

Similarly, these steps do not guarantee a result ... sometimes not only do the wants exclude each other but the needs also. You need space in a relationship, I need intimacy ... compromise may be the only way forward. These steps increase your choices and hence your effectiveness in managing differences.

However, the tennis coach can make some guarantees. Hit the ball with a good top spin two feet above the net and the ball will never go over the end line. The guarantee with these steps is that you will manage your differences in open and honest ways without argument or conflict. If you slip into argument or conflict, you have slipped off the steps!

Review questions

After you have used the steps you may wish to use one or more of these questions to achieve an even greater Win-Win.

'How important is the issue to you in 0-10?'
'How much do you feel I understand you 0-10?'

What do I need to do, so that you would feel I understand you even more?' (If there is a low score.)
'How much do you sense a willingness from me to meet your needs 0-10?'
'What do I need to do, so you would feel I was more willing to meet your needs?' (If there is a low score.)
'How good a solution is that for you 0-10?'
'How could it be an even better solution?' (If there is a low score.)

Steps to conflict resolution

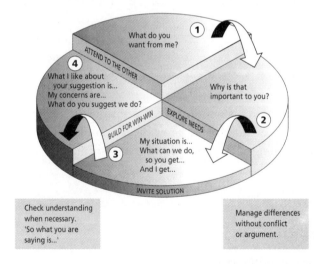

Check understanding when necessary. 'So what you are saying is...'

Manage differences without conflict or argument.

A good relationship requires mutual understanding and acceptance, not always agreement.

Chapter 8

Preventing Conflict

In this chapter:

♦ **preventing conflict**
♦ **the pitfalls of making assumptions and mind reading**
♦ **deal with the small cracks before they erupt**
♦ **see life through the eyes of the others**
♦ **take responsibility for your relationships, today.**

Rather than wait for the crisis moment before you attend to your relationship, review it when everything is running smoothly. After all, you get your car serviced even though it is running fine. You do this to prevent a breakdown. It's better to visit the dentist for a check up before you get toothache. Grow the relationship when the sun is shining! Take time out for the following:

♦ Review the relationship.
♦ Agree what is going well and what isn't.
♦ Discuss what matters most.

Make quality time

Making quality time for regular discussions can be the best way to clear up misunderstandings. With today's hectic lifestyle it is probably best to set aside some time, which is convenient for both of you, and keep to it. Use the skills to check with each other, giving both of you talking and listening time.

> People usually do the best they can with the resources they have.
> NLP presupposition

Difficult people

A lot of conflict arises simply because of the assumptions we make about others and the interpretations we put on the things said. Such conflicts could be defused by a few minutes of skilful and honest discussion.

Remember, if you find people difficult, they are likely to find you difficult too. You may want to explore and understand their intention before condemning their actions. Forgiveness is a decision and you may wish to ponder on the question 'Who gains most if you forgive ?'

Talk sooner rather than later

Avoid storing up resentment. As soon as you sense discomfort in the relationship, share your concern, even if the cause remains uncertain.

> I see you as wrong. You see me as wrong. We are both right. That's not logical but it is psychological.

Pete is becoming increasingly uncommunicative. He comes home from work and wants to be left alone in front of the TV to unwind. Kate feels excluded. The longer she leaves off talking to him, the more the resentment is likely to grow.

Leave it for days or even weeks and Kate will have plenty to say to Pete. *'You never talk to me any more. You take me for granted. All you ever do is work, watch TV and go out with your mates. You are turning out to be just like your father ...'* and it is not likely to stop there!

You are responsible for what you think.

Had she explained how she felt in the early stages, she wouldn't have been nearly so angry or as willing to blame him. *'Pete, I'm feeling distant from you and I am concerned.'*

People who are good at prevention, see trouble coming and do something about it early. You can stop trouble brewing by recognising the early warning signs and dealing with the minor incidents rather than wait till the full-blown crisis erupts.

Stay current
Avoid broadening the issue by bringing up the past *'You were just like that last Christmas ...'* or mind-reading into the future *'You'll never change ...'* Stay with the present and what you can change now. The past is the playing field of win-lose ... the present is the field of understanding and collaboration. The here and now can be changed. Beware of wasting time fighting over what can never be changed.

Think solutions
Offer a plan for improving things rather than merely complaining or venting your anger. Instead of smouldering because your partner comes home at different times each night and expects supper ready, voice your frustration. Explain that a call just before he leaves the office would solve this problem from your perspective and ask if this would work for him.

Change shoes

Imagine yourself in the other person's shoes.
How would it feel to be the other person at
this moment relating to you, hearing what
you are saying and seeing what you are
doing? Swap roles in the argument. Try

> People usually
> do the best
> they can with
> the resources
> they have.
> NLP
> presupposition

this in real life and invite your partner to do the same.
You might get a laugh by viewing yourself from the other
side … as well as improved understanding.

Avoid the pitfalls

Beware of personalising the problem. If you want help
with the washing up, it is unlikely that *'You never help
with the washing up'* will make him spring into action.
This is a quick way to start an *'I do my share.'* *'No you
don't.'* *'Yes I do'* argument.

When you put other person in the 'wrong', the argument
can go round in circles and even spirals.

Avoid quick jibes, *'If you call that being together at
breakfast, I'd rather you slept in!'* as she slams the kitchen
door. Such parting shots can leave a lingering poisonous
fallout. Avoid ending a session on a sour note.

If only

Wanting the other person to change is a common 'if
only' that most of us have said at some time in our lives.
'If only he'd think first.' *'If only she'd stop sulking.'* *'If only
… if only.'*

This attitude may put you in a passive, victim-like role. You are waiting for the other person to change, to make things all right for you. By sitting around in this passive way

> You are responsible for what you think.

you could be waiting a long time for things to improve and you could also be putting your life on hold. The pro active approach is likely to give you more choices and gain respect from the other person.

Playing to the crowd
Open arenas encourage playing to the crowd, taking sides and scoring points. Audiences have their place at sporting events … in win-lose situations. They don't belong in the arena of understanding. This is best achieved in private.

Name-calling
Insults and name-calling can be baits, drawing you away from win-win. To call someone a nagging bitch or a self-centred egotist is an attack likely to lead to retaliation rather than collaboration.

> You are responsible for what you say.

The impasse
Listen to each other. Show you understand each other. Recognize your needs are not always compatible. Agree to disagree and move on. A good relationship requires mutual understanding and acceptance, not necessarily agreement.

> You are responsible for what you do.

Beware the victim mode
People who whine and nag are less likely to have their real needs met than those who express them openly. Other people cannot read your mind, even

though they might try. If you want something badly you may have to come out and ask for it. You may need to replace *'Love is not having to ask'* with *'If I need to feel loved I need to tell you how.'*

> Silence is not always golden.

Language suggestions

Unhelpful	Replace with
You should ...	I need ...
You are ...	My perception is ...
Yes but ...	Yes and ...
Who is to blame ?	What can we do ... ?

Good luck!

Your relationships today may be where your thoughts and actions of the last few years have brought you. Your future relationships are being shaped by your thoughts and behaviours of today. What you choose to do today affects what you will have tomorrow. Today and now are the places to start. Good luck!

You may not be perfect, neither am I, so we could suit each other admirably.

Alexander Pope

What's Your Style?

Use this questionnaire to discover your preferences in managing conflict.

Imagine real conflict situations and think about how you tend to handle them. For each statement choose the response according to how often you tend to use that way of dealing with conflict.

		Never	Rarely	Sometimes	Often	Very Typical
		1	2	3	4	5
1	I try to get my own way					
2	I smooth things over and avoid the conflict					
3	I do what is necessary to have my ideas accepted					
4	I try to understand the other person's needs					
5	I let other people have their way					
6	I work with the other person to solve the problem					
7	I fight for my point of view					
8	I walk away from conflict situations					
9	I find a mid point between us					

Transfer your scores from each question onto the grid on page 120 and then total.

	Fight	Flight	Flow
1			
2			
3			
4			
5			
6			
7			
8			
9			
Total			

Treat your answers as a rough guide as there will be many variations on these three basic styles. It will be inaccurate to characterize anyone as having a single, rigid style for dealing with conflict. Each of us is capable of using all three styles and indeed, each of the styles will be useful in some situations. See Chapter 5 for a full explanation.

Resolution Route

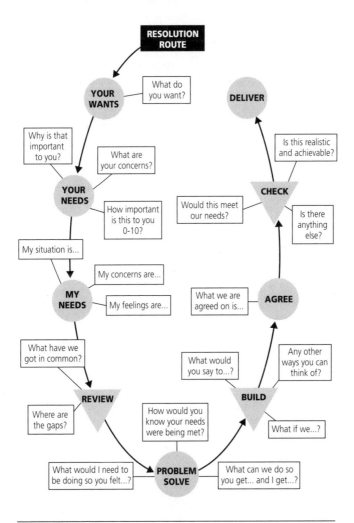

Handling Accusations

TWO VIEWS ARE BETTER THAN ONE

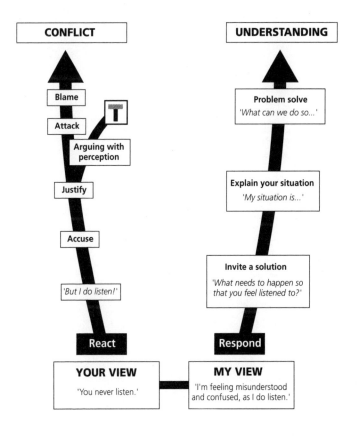

Group Conflict

The more people involved in a conflict, the more complex it will be to meet everyone's needs.

Complete a segment for each individual involved in the conflict and negotiate to an agreed solution, which is to be built from everyone's needs.

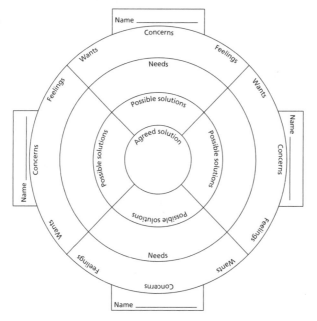

Start from the point of agreement rather than the disagreement.

Listen and Talk

Listen Acceptingly

1 For the moment, put to one side your concerns, feelings and needs.

2 Listen for what is important to the other person
   ◆ feelings – concerns – needs

3 Accept what the other person says *as true* for him
   ◆ resist argument
   ◆ Suspend judgement

4 Sum up what you have heard every few sentences
   ◆ *So what you are saying is...*
   ◆ *What I am hearing is...*
   ◆ *Anything else you want to add?*

5 You are not listening if you
   ◆ justify – argue – advise – interrupt

Talk Constructively

1 Talk about what you
   ◆ are feeling
   ◆ are concerned about
   ◆ see as your real needs

2 Use 'I' language
   ◆ *I feel...*
   ◆ *My concerns are...*
   ◆ *What I need is...*

3 Beware
   ◆ accusation – *You are always...*
   ◆ blame – *You make me feel...*
   ◆ demand – *You should...*

At a Glance

Meeting

Expectations
Concerns
Issues
Needs

Expectations
Concerns
Issues
Needs

Growing a Barrier

"What you don't realise is..."
"Yes but..."

'The problem with that is...'
'As I said...'

Expectations
Concerns
Issues
Needs

MOAN
ARGUE
RESIST
REJECT
ASSUME
JUSTIFY
DEMAND
INTERRUPT

Expectations
Concerns
Issues
Needs

Digging Yourself Into a Hole

MOAN
ARGUE
RESIST
REJECT
ASSUME
JUSTIFY
DEMAND
INTERRUPT
CONTRADICT
ACCUSE
PUT DOWN
MIND READ
JUDGE
BLAME
ADVISE
CRITICISE
THREATEN
BRING UP THE PAST
INTERPRET
GENERALSIE
PERSONALISE

'You should...'
'Any fool knows...'
'Your problem is...'

'You always...'
'You make me feel...'
'That's your fault...'

Expectations
Concerns
Issues
Needs

Expectations
Concerns
Issues
Needs

The Wider Picture

The higher you climb,
the more you'll see,
the broader the perspective,
the clearer the areas for agreement.

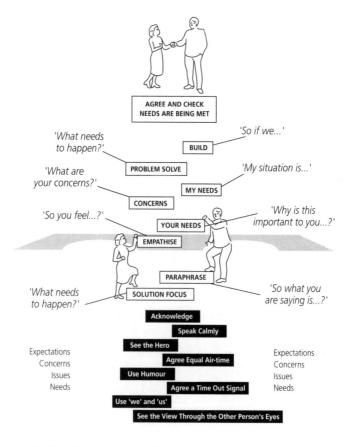

Rather than argue, problem solve on both sets of needs.

Case Study

As it was!

The problem

Staff turnover had been above the company average for months. Locally there was little unemployment so recruiting was difficult at the best of times. Losing staff mattered.

Unable to avoid facing it any longer, the situation was broached at a consultative council meeting, a relatively new process. Unsurprisingly perhaps, the reality of workplace, as experienced by employees, burst out. Was it surprising that people were leaving? The scathing language of rock bottom morale filled the room like an enormous driver's airbag exploding on impact.

One representative, Sue, said staff on her shift felt undervalued for all the effort they were putting in. Dave described graphically how he had made numerous suggestions but had not been listened to by even one manager. James and Alan both told of how it was common for their staff to be made to feel bad after getting things wrong, without ever being shown how to get it right in the first place.

So how come this depth of feeling had remained

concealed for so long? Well, why on earth would it come out if there was little hope of anyone taking notice? This, however, was an important first step… to acknowledge the problem, to ask some questions, "What's happening?" "What's life like for you out there?" And most importantly, to want to hear the answer, *their answer.*

All this sounds understandably important to people, so what is it they actually want?…. this part didn't take long either….. *"Some sort of recognition that we work damned hard would be a start". "An environment in which we can express how we feel without the risk of being labelled as moaners or troublemakers". "More flexibility by managers". "We want to be involved in decisions that affect us". "More scope for sharing ideas and concerns".* This all sounded reasonable, worryingly reasonable to Pat who was the relatively new senior manager chairing the meeting. 'Worrying' because these perfectly understandable wishes had seemingly been so elusive to these people. What was going on?

It would, of course, have been very easy at this stage for Pat to get locked into the urge to stand by her fellow managers, to close ranks. Thankfully she resisted. Equally, she didn't want to alienate her manager colleagues either after being 'at the helm' for such a short time. Conscious that she wasn't in a position to speak accurately on behalf of other managers, she got agreement for a meeting with managers and staff attending.

Attending to the other view

Rather than act as messenger of bad news, Pat sat down with her managers beforehand to check out the their view of how things were going and share her perception. She described observations of some very good areas of practice along with other things she wasn't so happy about. She displayed a chart showing the staff turnover figures in relation to the rest of the company – purely objective facts – and told the managers that she thought turnover could be reduced if the whole department faced the problem together. There was some reticence but all acknowledged that to just carry on as if everything was okay, doing nothing about it, was *not* an option. They agreed to the meeting and also agreed to begin by hearing what staff had to say…. after all it was them that were leaving!

Wanting to avoid a slanging match Pat spent considerable time in the days before the meeting encouraging all those involved to speak openly and honestly and, to listen carefully without getting defensive. She highlighted the damage that could be done by making *accusations* and *assumptions* about other people's intentions. The other key ingredient for this to work was to *check* that what they heard someone say was what the person actually meant.

Pat opened the meeting by putting things into context. She mentioned recent achievements, the hard graft by staff, the frustrations felt by managers, that some 'issues' had been raised by the consultative council, and the apparent desire by all to improve things. She gained immediate agreement. This was all real and true, as experienced by everyone in the room – a solid starting point. She went on to outline the concerns raised by the staff reps, checked with them that it was accurate, then bit by bit began to withdraw, letting others do the talking. Various staff members described how they felt.

Initially, it felt like a barrage and the managers' responses varied from silence to the inevitable outbursts of denial and defensiveness:

"That's all very well but that's only because…..".
Look, you knew what the job was like when you started…".

Before Pat had time to jump in, one of the management team saw where this was going and suggested to his colleagues that they all listen carefully. This, after all, was what people were experiencing and no amount of arguing would change it for them. He pointed back to the staff leaving figures still on the wall.

Flushing out unmet needs
Pat decided to probe a bit deeper to check out staff needs, *"Why are these things so important to you?"*

The answers she got served to lift the lid off the box, homogeneously labelled 'staff', but which actually contained a whole range of very different, individual, emotional human beings. What apparently amounted to a generalized desire to be valued, in fact, unfolded into a whole *variety* of unmet needs.

Sue, for example, said she needed to know her team felt good and were 'looked after' – contented staff are productive staff. She also felt torn. On the one hand she wanted to be seen as a solid company person, a good shift leader on the other, she empathised with the frustrations of her staff and found it hard to rationalize the management line she was expected to take. Dave described something different. He quite accepted that his ideas might be considered and turned down if they were not possible but to be dismissed out of hand as if he was some irritating schoolboy 'boffin' beggared belief. For James, it was important to feel competent at whatever he did. He didn't mind being trained and coached, but to be set up to fail was almost intolerable. Another person added that for her it was simply about needing to be treated like a sensible adult with a genuine interest in her work and with something to offer. She also thought a bit more 'give and take' would go a long way to let her know that someone had noticed how much extra time she'd put in. An off-the-shelf quick fix wasn't about to meet these diverse needs.

Martin, one of the managers, made the point that deadlines were tight and things often had to happen quickly, so there wasn't always time to discuss how things were done, especially when staffing was short. The staff response was direct but measured, *"If folk felt better about their 'lot' at work, short staffing wouldn't be such a problem and if we were treated better we'd be more likely to want to and, be able to help."*

"So what do you suggest we do?" Pat visibly smiled when she heard her most junior manager ask this gem.

Inviting solutions

In a flash came the first suggestion. To make sure time was spent when a person first joined the company, training and helping them to do the job properly, giving them maximum chance to succeed, and then to keep reminding them how well they're doing. Pat wanted to capitalise on this so asked managers if there was any reason why that wasn't possible. *"Apart from us being bogged down in paperwork and rushed off our feet you mean?"* A predictable retort perhaps, but nevertheless a valid one for managers. *"Tell you what,"* Martin said to Pat, *"You look hard at a more efficient method for doing managers monthly reports and we'll build in regular time for coaching and short supervision meetings".*

A price worth paying, thought Pat, *if* it met staff needs. She found not only agreement but, for such a relatively small achievement, a disproportionate air of appreciation, almost enjoyment, that at last someone was listening and prepared to do something.

Other issues were raised, for example, what could be gained by involving staff in decisions about things that affected them and the effect the way managers spoke to people had on them – a revelation in itself to most managers. Pat was gratified by the way in which this potential keg of dynamite was not only generating solutions but also becoming a relatively non-threatening and even comfortable process.

Naturally, not all problems were solved but 'trenches' were being filled in, barbed wire removed, and this was a great start for what was bound to become a continuing process.

Review Comments

In looking at the case study, it will become obvious that conflict, spoken or unspoken, existed because needs were not being met.

This was not because of ill will or deliberate sabotage on the part of mangers or staff, but for very human reasons, lack of time and lack of understanding of needs.

We all tend to live in our own model of the world, managing our behaviours from our own values and beliefs. In this naïve state, we also tend to believe that our model of the world is the 'right one', and we make our value judgements from that position.

When we begin to use the simple processes outlined in this book, we begin also to discover the needs of others, what is driving them, and what is important to them from their value 'planet'. We discover that men are not just from Mars and women from Venus, but that some men live on Venus, some women on Mars and many of us live on neighbouring planets or we have houses on each of the planets. Our planet is determined by our core values, which govern our behaviours, our language and our source of happiness.

In accepting people as being different, in understanding their different needs, in expressing our own and being prepared to negotiate so both of us get what is important to us, we discover the magic of win-win.

Bibliography

Bolton R., *People Skills*, Prentice-Hall, 1986

Booher D., *How to Say it Right First Time*, McGraw-Hill, 1994

Cornelius H. and Faire S., *Everyone Can Win*, Simon Schuster, 1989

Covey R., *The 7 Habits of Highly Effective People*, Simon Schuster, 1989

Dana D., *Talk It Out*, Kogan Page, 1990

Elgin S., *How to Disagree Without Being Disagreeable*, John Wiley, 1997

Stone D., Patton B., Heen S., *Difficult Conversations*, Michael Joseph, 1999

Quinn M. and T., *Couple Alive*, Family Caring Trust, 1998.

Ury W., *Getting Past No*, Business Books Ltd, 1991

Further Reading from How To Books

2-4-6-8 How Do You Communicate?
Phillip Khan-Panni, 2001

365 Steps to Self-Confidence
David Lawrence-Preston, 2001

From Blank Page to First Draft in 15 Minutes
Phillip Khan-Panni, 2001

Grow Your Own Achievers
Lesley Morrissey, 2002

Managing Difficult People
Karen Mannering, 2001

Say it with Pictures
Dr Harry Alder, 2001

Train Your Team Yourself
Lisa Hadfield-Law, 2002

Writing Speaking, Listening
Helen Wilkie, 2001

For comprehensive information on How To Books' titles
visit How To Books on line at **www.howtobooks.co.uk**

For further information on Shay and Margaret's consultancy group, *People First*, and their range of products and workshops contact:

Tel: (+44) 1425 612610

www.PeopleFirst-Intl.com